Toward the
Kingdom of Heaven

Toward the Kingdom of Heaven:

40 Daily Readings on the Sermon on the Mount

Toward the Kingdom of Heaven

978-1-7910-0915-1

978-1-7910-0916-8 *eBook*

Sermon on the Mount:
A Beginner's Guide to the Kingdom of Heaven

978-1-5018-9989-8

978-1-5018-9990-4 *eBook*

Sermon on the Mount: DVD

978-1-5018-9993-5

Sermon on the Mount: Leader Guide

978-1-5018-9991-1

978-1-5018-9992-8 *eBook*

Also by Amy-Jill Levine

Entering the Passion of Jesus: A Beginner's Guide to Holy Week
Light of the World: A Beginner's Guide to Advent

AMY-JILL LEVINE

TOWARD
the
KINGDOM
of
HEAVEN

40 DAILY READINGS
on the
SERMON *on the* MOUNT

Abingdon Press / Nashville

Toward the Kingdom of Heaven
40 Daily Readings on the Sermon on the Mount

Library of Congress Control Number: 2020941646

978-1-7910-0915-1

20 21 22 23 24 25 26 27 28 29 — 10 9 8 7 6 5 4 3 2 1
MANUFACTURED IN THE UNITED STATES OF AMERICA

For
Mike Glenn
Rubel Shelly
Rob Simbeck

And with gratitude to
Randy Horick

CONTENTS

INTRODUCTION

From its opening verse, "When Jesus saw the crowds, he went up the mountain; and after he sat down, his disciples came to him" (Matthew 5:1) to the beginning of the sermon, "Blessed are the poor in spirit, for theirs is the kingdom of heaven" (Matthew 5:3), to Jesus's closing words about the houses on firm and weak foundations, to the crowd's astonished reaction, the Sermon on the Mount beckons to us in multiple ways.

Its evocations of the Scriptures of Israel (what would be called the Old Testament) show us how Jesus both interprets and fulfills the Law (the Torah) and the Prophets, and so it cannot be understood fully unless we see that continuity with Abraham, Moses, and David.

Its comforting Beatitudes lead inexorably to its challenging ethics, all the while providing disciples the assurance that they really can be the light of the world and the salt of the earth. Its ability to get to the heart of the commandments—do not murder becomes do not be angry; do not commit adultery becomes do not lust—begins the discussion of how the body and the mind must work together. So, too, its teachings against hypocrisy help us to engage in needed introspection for getting the logs out of our own eyes.

Perhaps the best-known part of the Sermon on the Mount is the "Our Father" prayer. With attention to the meaning of the Greek, and suggestions concerning the underlying Hebrew or Aramaic, we can hear these ancient words anew. In so doing, we see both how they are connected to the rest of Jesus's teaching and how they touch upon the world as it should be.

But the prayer is not the only familiar passage. Hearing with fresh ears the implications of "Love your enemies," "Do not let your left hand know what your right hand is doing," and "Consider the lilies of the field," and so many more familiar phrases not only brings Jesus's teaching to life, it shows them as a guide by which we might live into the kingdom of heaven.

Each verse, even each word, opens up to ever new interpretations. When the verses are put into dialogue with the rest of the Gospels, and the rest of the Bible, more insights emerge. We draw out connections between the Sermon in Matthew 5–7 and themes sounded elsewhere in Matthew, such as the concerns for righteousness, resisting temptation, and creating the beloved community where both justice and mercy reside.

These daily readings put Jesus's comments in the Sermon into conversation with the Scriptures of Israel, with the other Gospels, with the epistles of Paul, and then they move from antiquity to today. To understand what a text means for us, it helps to understand what it meant to the people who first heard it. These readings, designed for daily reflection and personal study, use the words of the Sermon to help us think about our own lives: parenting and children, economics and business, politics and democracy, have versus need, the gap between the way things are and the way things should be, and what we can do to mind that gap.

The best teachers—and Jesus was certainly one of the best teachers the world has known—do more than convey information. They find ways of using language to encourage their students to think and then to act. They teach not only by providing answers but by helping their students ask the right questions. They know that they will never have the last word, and they take a certain pride when their students bring what they've learned into conversation with other books, other experiences, and other times and cultures. The Sermon on the Mount is just such a teaching: it raises new questions and new interpretations. When studied with attention to history, language, culture, and ethics, it turns from a series of well-known phrases into a beginner's guide to the kingdom of heaven.

These daily readings are here to accompany you on what Jesus calls the "hard road" through the "narrow gate," both to keep you from getting offtrack and to point out the birds and the lilies—the inspiration and the challenge—along the way. Your first step is to open your Bibles to Matthew chapter 5. God willing, it won't be your last step.

THE TEACHER
IS HERE

Readings:
Deuteronomy 6:6-9; Psalm 25;
Matthew 4:23; Acts 2:42

*Jesus went throughout Galilee, teaching in their synagogues and
proclaiming the good news of the kingdom....*

Matthew 4:23a

The title "sermon" suggests many things. Positive connotations
include inspirational, comforting, and challenging. More negative
associations include boring, preachy, and irrelevant. I discovered,
after giving a sermon in a Protestant church one Sunday morning
(I can't "proclaim" the gospel, so someone else read the text, but I
can certainly talk about it), that "sermon" is not always associated
with "instruction" or with "time to discover something new about an
old text." One elderly gentleman told me at the end of the service, "I
learned more about the gospel this morning than I have heard in the
past sixty years."

I worry about Sunday sermons that don't offer new insight into
the text. Sermons that use a single term from the biblical passage to
speak about something unrelated to that same passage annoy me.
Sermons that have nothing to do with the text or, horror of horrors,
consist of someone else's poetry, find me parsing Hebrew verbs to
keep from either complaining out loud or falling asleep.

These same concerns hold for the rabbi's *derasha* (Hebrew for
homily) or *d'var Torah* (Hebrew: "a word of Torah") in the synagogue
as well. If you think that parts of the lectionary drag, don't complain:

my rabbi has to offer remarks both relevant and new to say about some of the more arcane passages in Leviticus and Numbers every year, and every year, he manages. He has more than 2,000 years of commentary from which to draw, and then he adds his own interpretation to this tradition. Consequently, I learn from his sermons more about the biblical text, how it has been interpreted in past generations, and what it may say to the present.

While a sermon is not the same thing as a classroom lecture, the genres are related. Matthew introduces the Sermon on the Mount with, "Then he began to speak, and taught them, saying…" (Matthew 5:2). The sermon closes with the crowd's reaction: they "were astounded at his teaching" (Matthew 7:28).

The Gospels portray Jesus as Messiah, miracle worker, healer, good news proclaimer, charismatic figure, and even "rock star" (a term of recent vintage used by some Christians to describe Jesus's relationship with the adoring crowds). "Teacher" is not the first response my students give when I ask them to describe Jesus. Nor, by the way, is "teacher" the first response from most five-year-olds to the question, "What do you want to be when you grow up?"

Yet throughout the Gospels, Jesus teaches. It's the first word Matthew (4:23) uses to describe his activity in Galilee. We find the same description in Matthew 9:35: "Then Jesus went about all the cities and villages, teaching in their synagogues…." In chapter 15, Matthew again shows Jesus teaching disciples and crowds; chapter 26, the account of Jesus's arrest, notes that Jesus was teaching every day in the Temple. When Jesus arrives in Bethany after the death of his friend Lazarus, Martha tells her sister Mary, "The Teacher is here" (John 11:28).

In Jewish tradition, studying religious texts is a form of worship; hence, synagogues are often calls *shuls*– from the Yiddish word for "school" (you can hear in the term the connection to the German

Schule). One "learns" the texts often with a study partner, so mutual instruction is also part of worship. The Hebrew root often translated "teach" is *l-m-d*: a disciple or a student in Hebrew is a *talmid*; the compendium of Jewish law and tradition is the *Talmud*.

In Deuteronomy 6, Moses presents the *shema (Hebrew for "hear!" or "listen!")*—which contains the commandment to love God with all one's being—as something "the LORD your God charged me to teach" (*laméd*, 6:1). In turn, the Psalms frequently ask God to provide instruction: "Make me to know your ways, O LORD; teach me (*lamdeni*) your paths; Lead me in your truth, and teach me (*lamdeni*), for you are the God of my salvation; for you I wait all day long" (Psalm 25:4-5).

There is always more to learn, whether about the Bible, science, or human nature. When we learn something new about the biblical text—perhaps a detail about translation or the notice of where the same terms are used; a fresh insight; an historical tidbit; a different way of understanding a familiar passage—there is delight for both the mind and the soul. Worship with the heart and soul need not be disengaged from thinking with the head. Teaching and learning, especially done in a community where questions are posed and alternative interpretations are welcome, are signs of the kingdom of heaven in our midst.

FULFILLING SCRIPTURE

2

Then Isaiah said: "Hear then, O house of David! Is it too little for you to weary mortals, that you weary my God also? Therefore the Lord himself will give you a sign. Look, the young woman is with child and shall bear a son, and shall name him Immanuel."

Isaiah 7:13-14

Matthew's Gospel is filled with fulfillment language. We see it in the very first chapter, when Matthew connects Jesus's birth to words that Isaiah spoke seven centuries earlier to King Ahaz of Judah. Ahaz was worried about external threats from two neighboring kingdoms (their cousins from the Northern Kingdom of Israel among them), and Isaiah reassures him that God will deliver a sign of God's presence and protection. The Hebrew text speaks of a pregnant young woman who will bear a son and she will name him Immanuel. The prophecy does not stop here. Isaiah continues: "He shall eat curds and honey by the time he knows how to refuse the evil and choose the good. For before the child knows how to refuse the evil and choose the good, the land before whose two kings you are in dread will be deserted" (Isaiah 7:15-16). In the Septuagint, the Greek translation of the Hebrew texts, the "young woman who is pregnant" becomes a "virgin who will conceive."

When Jesus's followers reread their Bibles—whether the Hebrew or (for Paul, Matthew, and the rest of the writers of what became the New Testament) the Septuagint—they saw Jesus throughout. For them, the prophets pointed to Jesus; Matthew in particular emphasizes the connections. Jesus's birth fulfills Micah's words that Bethlehem, King David's city, would produce a shepherd-ruler for the people. The return from Egypt fulfills what Hosea, in a different context, said about the Israelite people (while also connecting Jesus to Moses—another connection Matthew doesn't want us to miss). Jesus's ministry in Galilee, Matthew points out, was "so that what had been spoken through the prophet Isaiah might be fulfilled" (Matthew 4:14). The people of Galilee who "sat in darkness" under the rule of Herod Antipas and in the shadow of Rome (as they sat under Assyrian occupation in Isaiah's time) would receive deliverance.

Matthew uses this same Greek verb for fulfill (*plēroō*) in the context of Jesus's healing miracles (8:17); his instruction to the crowds "not to make him known" (12:16-17); and his use of parables (13:35). We see it at his arrest, when Jesus tells those with him that his fate is to fulfill scripture. Mark also uses it when he writes: "The time is fulfilled and the kingdom of God has come near; repent, and believe in the good news" (1:15).

Jesus uses this same verb in the Sermon on the Mount: "Do not think that I have come to abolish the law or the prophets; I have come not to abolish but to fulfill" (Matthew 5:17). The expression "to fulfill" can also mean to make complete or to perfect. When it comes to fulfilling the Law, Jesus by no means does away with it. To the contrary, he means showing his disciples how best to bring the Law to life, to enact it, and to live it.

What does that look like? When the imprisoned John the Baptist dispatches some of his disciples to ask Jesus if he is "the one who is to come" (Luke 7:20), Jesus tells them to tell John what they have seen: the blind receive their sight, the lame walk, people with leprosy are healed, and the poor hear the good news. We can speculate on what that good news is: perhaps that the poor will receive comfort in heaven, or, more likely, that the rich will truly follow what they have already been commanded to do: "If there is among you anyone in need, a member of your community in any of your towns within the land that the LORD your God is giving you, do not be hard-hearted or tight-fisted toward your needy neighbor.... Since there will never cease to be some in need on the earth, I therefore command you, 'Open your hand to the poor and needy neighbor in your land'" (Deuteronomy 15:7, 11).

Much the same formulation is used in Isaiah 61, which Jesus reads in his hometown synagogue (Luke 4) and then announces, "Today this scripture has been fulfilled in your hearing" (v. 21).

How do we bring the Law to life—to fulfillment—in our own lives? Jesus's teaching from the mountaintop is a primer on that topic. Bring healing to those who suffer in body and mind. Be generous rather than stingy; be grateful rather than resentful. Be poor in spirit and so recognize the gap between what you have and what others need, between the way things are and the way things should be. Be meek and don't lord it over others. Hunger for righteousness and feed the hungry. Be a peacemaker. Be salt that makes life taste good for everyone. Be a light for others. Be reconciled to each other. Love enemies as God's children. Trust God to provide. Paul states, "Love does no wrong to a neighbor; therefore, love is the fulfilling of the law" (Romans 13:10). When we fulfill Torah, then we will be fulfilled.

JESUS, TORAH, AND TRADITION

3

Reading:
Matthew 15:2

"Why do your disciples break the tradition of the elders? For they do not wash their hands before they eat."

Matthew 15:2

All laws require updating. We can't run the United States today on the original language of the Constitution; we have Amendments for multiple good reasons.

Jews also know that laws needed updating. The treatment of slaves in Deuteronomy updates the laws in Leviticus; concerns for how to run a temple become spiritualized when the community lacks a temple—whether under Babylonian exile in the sixth century BCE or after 70 CE, when Rome burned down the Second Temple. The people who wrote the Dead Sea Scrolls had their own take on how to understand the Torah, as did Philo, the first-century Jewish philosopher from Alexandria. Pharisees and Sadducees; the followers of John the Baptist; the Zealots; the people in the synagogue of Nazareth; the schools of Hillel and Shammai whose debates are recorded in rabbinic texts: all had their interpretations. Jesus is being a normal Jewish individual living in a Jewish community when he offers his understanding of God's instructions.

As presented by Matthew, the Pharisees are Jesus's major competitors in interpreting the Torah. The reason why Jesus and the Pharisees debate is not because they are diametrically opposed to each other; it is because they agree on the importance of both under-standing what the Torah says and how to put that understanding into practice. The Torah is the guide for the people of Israel—not just the high priests, not just in Jerusalem, but also in the countryside, in Galilee and in the Diaspora. What does God want us to do? How do we live as a community? How do we sanctify our lives?

The Pharisees had the "tradition of the elders," which is con-nected to what rabbinic texts call the "Oral Torah." The rabbinic text *Pirke Avot*, the "Ethics of the Fathers," begins with the notice that this interpretive tradition was also revealed at Mt. Sinai. Many biblical texts require such traditions. For example, when a Christian denomination reads 1 Corinthians 11:24—"and when he had given thanks, he broke it and said, 'This is my body that is for you. Do this in remembrance of me'"—it is tradition that determines who gets to speak the words, which type of bread, how the congregation receives the bread, how often they receive the bread, who can participate in this ritual, and how they understand it. Not surprisingly, different churches have different interpretations.

Matthew reports on a debate between Jesus and a group of Pharisees and scribes who had come to Galilee from Jerusalem to ask why Jesus's disciples did not wash their hands before eating. From their point of view, applying to village life practices followed by priests in the Temple was answering God's call to be a "priestly king-dom and a holy nation" (Exodus 19:6). They were extending priestly privilege to everyone and so giving everyone a new way of sanctifying their lives. Jesus then changes the subject to that of other interpreta-tions of the Torah.

Just as the rabbinic tradition sent Moses back up onto the mountain, Matthew takes this very Jewish way of understanding the Torah and shows Jesus, the new Moses, teaching his disciples how to interpret this text. Jesus and the Pharisees agree on the importance of the Torah; they disagree on its interpretation. The same point holds among Christian denominations: all agree that the Sermon on the Mount is important; they disagree on how to interpret it.

We can think of the Sermon on the Mount as a form of Jesus's Oral Torah, but instead of the tradition of the elders—a tradition informed by a community who themselves debated how best to follow the Torah and generally reached consensus—the Sermon is Jesus's own tradition. That's why, at the end of the Sermon on the Mount, the listeners are astounded. They remark that he teaches with authority, not like the scribes. In other words, he's not relying on that oral tradition or community discussion. He's relying on his own views of how he thinks the Torah ought to be interpreted.

These different approaches open questions for us. Do we follow an individual who speaks with authority or do we sort out answers in community conversation? Do we read as literalists or do we do what Jesus and the Pharisees did: read and interpret with attention to our own settings? Do we seek new ways of sanctifying daily life or do we find comfort in the ways we learned as children?

The same dynamic plays out today in debates among Christians over such topics as homosexuality or the ordination of women. It played out in the past on debates concerning the meaning of the Eucharist, the authority of bishops, even the nature of the Trinity. From both the Pharisees and Jesus we can find guidance. From the Pharisees, about whom Jesus says, "'The scribes and the Pharisees sit on Moses' seat; therefore, do whatever they teach you and follow it'" (Matthew 23:2-3a), we learn the importance of community debate, of updating, of both attending to tradition and modifying it when necessary; from Jesus, we learn the importance of the individual voice, a voice that speaks compellingly about the heart of the Torah.

JESUS AND THE
NEW COMMUNITY

While he was still speaking to the crowds, his mother and his brothers were standing outside, wanting to speak to him. Someone told him, "Look, your mother and your brothers are standing outside, wanting to speak to you." But to the one who had told him this, Jesus replied, "Who is my mother, and who are my brothers?" And pointing to the disciples, he said, "Here are my mother and my brothers! For whoever does the will of my Father in heaven is my brother and sister and mother."

Matthew 12:46-50

For Jesus, the disciples represent the beginnings of the *ekklesia*. That's the Greek word for *assembly*. It comes into Spanish as *iglesia*, which is pronounced much like the Greek, and into English usually as "church." The Greek meaning *assembly* gets us closer to understanding what Jesus is trying to convey. Jesus is not setting up a building with a steeple, apse, nave, and social hall. He is speaking rather of a community, a group with shared interests, a new family.

In the Septuagint, the Greek translation of the Hebrew Bible, *ekklesia* is the translation of the Hebrew term *qahal*—the assembly of Israel. It means the entire community. In Deuteronomy, Moses reminds the people of the commandments God gave them "on the day of the assembly (*qahal*)" (10:4). In Numbers, when the people threaten to return to Egypt, Moses and Aaron fall on their faces before the entire assembly (*qahal*). 1 Kings 8:22 states, "Then Solomon stood before the altar of the LORD in the presence of all the assembly (*qahal*) of Israel, and spread out his hands to heaven." 1 Kings 8:55 adds, "he stood and blessed all the assembly (*qahal*) of Israel with a loud voice." The *qahal*, the *ekklesia*, for Israel, is "we, the people"—the entire community.

Jesus's twelve disciples therefore remind us of the original twelve tribes, those who stood at Mt. Sinai and those who worshiped at Solomon's Temple. There is an appealing symmetry to this connection of the disciples to Israel and Israel then to the church, but Jesus intends for us to go much further than symbolism. While he is teaching the crowds, someone interrupts to let him know that his mother and brothers are waiting outside (Mark 3:32 adds that his sisters were there as well); the implication is that he should stop what he is doing immediately and go to his family. Instead, he reprioritizes; he redefines family (and so community) first as his disciples, then as "whoever does the will of my Father in heaven."

This new *ekklesia* is an alternative community, an alternative family not defined primarily by blood ties, tribe, nationality, or political loyalty (whether to Rome or to another empire, then or now), but by the commitment to do God's will. The new community is endlessly inclusive; anyone who does the work of the Creator is a member.

What is that work? Jesus spells it out in his beginner's guide to the kingdom.

The Sermon on the Mount becomes a good standard for a healthy church, which is a community and not primarily a building. Healthy churches should model love of neighbor. Of course they should model reconciliation, empathy, and mutual support. But they are healthier still when they live into Jesus's teaching about family—when they bring to life the new community defined not by labels or prior loyalties, not even defined by confessions or denominations, not by anything but by doing the will of our common Father.

BLESSED ARE THE CHRIST-PUSHERS

Readings:
John 15:18-25; Matthew 5:11-12; Acts 17:1-15

5

*"If the world hates you, be aware that it hated me before it hated you.
If you belonged to the world, the world would love you as its own."*
                                                                            John 15:18-19

For people in that first generation after Jesus, being called a "Christian" probably would have been an insult. It is not uncommon for groups to take their name from what was originally an insult used by their opponents. The most obvious example of this phenomenon is the label "Protestant," a term initially used negatively by representatives of the Roman Catholic Church to refer to those who followed Reformation views. The Reformers themselves, such as Luther and Calvin, did not originally call themselves Protestants.

Being known as a follower of Jesus, especially in the Gentile areas evangelized by Paul, was a problem. Those early disciples were politically suspect. Everyone knew that Jews were not going to worship Rome's gods. But Gentiles who turned from their parents' and their cities' religious practices to worship the God of Israel were traitors to the state and betrayers of the family.

In the Sermon on the Mount, the final beatitude Jesus gives is: "Blessed are you when people revile you and persecute you and utter all kinds of evil against you falsely on my account" (Matthew 5:11). Matthew, who records Jesus's story, is honest about the difficulties being a disciple can create. If one puts the family of faith ahead of one's parents or spouse, the name-calling begins. If one insists on loving enemies, problems may ensue. If one announces that a man put to death by the Roman state is now reigning in heaven, the state might have some concerns. And if one acts in a way that locals consider to be unpatriotic, persecution is likely.

New movements also risk negative reactions from people who do not understand them. For example, after Paul and Silas proclaimed Jesus as the Messiah in Thessalonika, some local ruffians accused them of being the "people who have been turning the world upside down" (Acts 17:6). Later, in front of the Roman procurator Felix, a local lawyer accuses Paul of being a pest, "an agitator," and a "ringleader" of a sect (Acts 24:5).

The term "Christian" only shows up in the New Testament three times, and in relatively late texts. It occurs twice in Acts (11:26; 26:28), a work likely dating to the early decades of the second century. It also appears in 1 Peter 4:16, and here we see the problem associated with the label: "Yet if any of you suffers as a Christian, do not consider it a disgrace, but glorify God because you bear this name." Once labeled "Christians," disciples were at risk. They were denying the local gods; they were eschewing the local religious practices. As if that were not bad enough, false stories were told about them. This is what happens to minority groups.

Christos is the Greek word for someone who is anointed. To Gentiles, calling someone *Christos* made no sense; they might think, "You're following an anointed one? You're following some guy with oil on him?" Perhaps that is why, as we learn from Acts, that Jesus's earliest followers did not called themselves by the title they gave their Lord. They called themselves followers of "the Way." The Greek for "way" is *hodos*; it's where we get the term "odometer," our mileage indicator. The term *Christian* arrived relatively late, and it was a label that was applied to the believers in Antioch (modern Antakya in Turkey, near the border with Syria).

Jesus teaches that being reviled inevitably comes with the territory for those who follow him. Reviling sometimes occurs when people associate the term *Christian* (or specifically "Catholic" or "Evangelical") with intolerance, with a particular political party, or with hatred of people who do not worship the same way that the majority does.

If one is to be reviled, one should be reviled for good reason. I'd like to see the term *Christian* associated with people who work for the humane treatment of all God's children, even if that means protesting certain governmental policies. I'd like to see the term associated with people who advocate for those who face food insecurity and lack of healthcare, even if that advocacy means some negative looks from others who insist that poverty is the fault of the individual person who is poor. People who act in ways that upset the status quo for the sake of loving one another may become reviled—Jesus knew that. And he also knew that they, in particular, are blessed.

THE RIGHTEOUSNESS OF THE PHARISEES?

6

Readings:
Luke 12:41-8; Matthew 5:18-20

For I tell you, unless your righteousness exceeds that of the scribes and Pharisees, you will never enter the kingdom of heaven.

Matthew 5:20

For many Christians, reading that Jesus's followers must uphold a higher standard of righteousness than the Pharisees creates cognitive dissonance. Since the Gospels, particularly Matthew, accuse the Pharisees of everything from hypocrisy to plotting the death of Jesus, readers may well conclude that Jesus is setting the bar at the lowest rung. If the Pharisees set the standard, then pretty much everyone can surpass it. To draw this conclusion, however, is to misunderstand who the Pharisees were.

Setting Pharisaic behavior as the minimum is by no means setting a ridiculously low standard. If they were that horrid, Paul (Philippians 3:5) would not boast about his being a member of the group. Josephus, a first-century Jewish historian, tells us that the Pharisees were popular teachers known for their mutual friendship (*Jewish War* 2:166), "conduct of reason," respect for their elders, their belief that people enjoy the free will to choose whether or not to follow the path of virtue, and their view that people will be judged on their behavior (*Antiquities* 18:12-15). Josephus also tells us that the Pharisees lived a simple life: basically, they both walked the walk and talked the talk. He further suggests—and this has direct relevance to the Sermon on the Mount—that the Pharisees were popular because their traditions of Torah interpretation "alleviated the harsher prescriptions of the Bible in civil and criminal law" (*Antiquities* 13:294). They were interpreters and updaters.

Some Christians claim that the Pharisees were separated from the community because the name "Pharisee" derives from the Hebrew root meaning "to separate," and thus the Pharisees were an elitist, self-segregating group. The etymology is possible but not secure. The connotation of elitist separatists is incorrect, for as Josephus notes, they are not separated from others but seek to teach others. The name "Pharisee" could also derive from a Hebrew root meaning "to specify" or "to be accurate," for the Pharisees were interested in how best to interpret the Torah.

We've already seen how Pharisees were trying to extend the holiness found in the Jerusalem Temple to all the people so that Israel could truly be a "priestly kingdom and a holy nation" (Exodus 19:6), language that gets repeated in 1 Peter 2:9 with its proclamation that the followers of Jesus are "a chosen race, a royal priesthood, a holy nation." For example, just as priests in the Temple washed their hands before touching any of the sacred elements, so Pharisees apparently suggested that everyone should wash their hands before eating an ordinary meal. That way, everyone would be like priests eating in the Temple. In so doing, every meal would be a sacred occasion and everyone eating would take the time to remember God. Thus, inherited status (since to be a priest in Judaism is a role determined by one's father) is less important than the actions we individually choose to take.

Jesus honors most of the Pharisaic teaching. He doesn't agree with all of it. He has his own way of interpreting the Torah. So did the Essenes, the Sadducees, the followers of John the Baptist, and numerous other groups in first-century Jewish life. Indeed, Pharisees also disagreed with each other. While Jesus rejects this type of hand washing as unnecessary, a vestige of this practice—as well as of the priestly ritual washing—occurs in those churches where the person presiding at the altar symbolically washes his or her hands before touching the bread or wafer that represents the body of the Christ.

The key word in Jesus's comment about the Pharisees here is *righteousness*, a term appearing often in Matthew's Gospel. When Matthew describes Joseph as a "righteous man" (1:19), he points to an individual who could have humiliated Mary by making their divorce a public spectacle—she's pregnant; they're engaged; the child is not his—but he chooses to divorce her quietly. Matthew even leaves clues about where else righteousness can be found. The first woman the New Testament mentions is Tamar (Matthew 1:3), who risked her life in order to become pregnant with Judah's child. Judah states, "She's more righteous than I am" (Genesis 38:26 CEB). Righteous individuals not only go the proverbial extra mile; they risk reputations, even lives, to do what is right.

Jesus is saying: "The Pharisees have the tradition of the elders. They have volunteered to live lives of holiness. Because of that, we expect more from them." How much more, then, would Jesus expect of his disciples?

LOVE AS RISK

If your enemies are hungry, give them bread to eat; and if they are thirsty, give them water to drink.

Proverbs 25:21

When Jesus says, "Love your enemies and pray for those who persecute you" (Matthew 5:44), he is evoking Proverbs even as his statement has a proverbial ring to it. Proverbs does not command love for enemies, but it moves in that direction. Proverbs insists: Don't be joyful when something bad happens to an enemy (the technical term for this reaction is *Schadenfreude*). Give them something to eat if they are hungry, and give them something to drink if they are thirsty; you would want them to do the same for you. Jesus is also evoking Genesis, since all people, even one's enemies, are in the image and likeness of God.

Jesus, teaching about a higher level of righteousness than the minimum requirement of civility and even than the merciful requirement of Proverbs, tells his disciples that they have to love their enemies. Why? Because this is what God does. God, who makes the sun shine on the evil and the good alike, acts with mercy and love to all. So if one is to be fully human, if one is to be complete (Greek: *telios*, sometimes translated *perfect* [see Matthew 5:48]), then act as God acts.

Today we have lost the rudiments of civility: it is easier to shout at our opponents than to engage in a civil conversation. Insulting language and *ad hominem* attacks are easier than rational argument and points backed up with data. Why listen to the scientists or those with actual credentials when anyone with an internet connection can become a self-proclaimed expert?

There are steps we can take toward manifesting this difficult kind of love. For example, we can be civil to the people with whom we substantially disagree. Be civil to the people who insult us. Be civil to the people who call us deplorable or think we're worthless or lazy. Do not respond to anger with anger. Do not respond to insult with insult. Respond with love. Join the protest, for in fact there are no innocent bystanders when the cry for justice goes unheeded, but we cannot demonize those who hold different views than ours.

If we do not respond with the grace that God shows us, Jesus goes on to say to his disciples, you're no better than the tax collectors whom you regard as enemies and traitors. If you love only those who already love you, and greet only those who already are part of the family, Jesus says, in effect, "Big deal." But if you want to be part of this new community, if you want to live by the Torah and into the kingdom, aim higher.

Jesus shows love to those the community in general despises. He dines with tax collectors: people who chose to work with Rome, the conquering empire; they chose to support the army that conquered them by taking funds from the local population. Just as bad, Jesus dines with "sinners." The term does not mean someone who eats non-kosher food, and it is not a general title for all people, since all people sin. No, these "sinners" are the people who seek personal gratification at the expense of the community. They are the ancient equivalents of drug pushers, arms dealers, inside traders, and loan sharks. They are "enemies of society," as it were. And Jesus eats with them.

As he does so, we can picture him calling these people to repentance, to restored relations with the community, toward the narrow path of righteousness rather than the wide road of personal gain.

Loving the enemy does not mean giving the enemy *carte blanche* to hurt us or our loved ones. Loving the enemy should not create situations where we put our families or friends in danger. But such love may, on occasion, put us in danger. Talking with the person on the other side of the picket line, the one who stands for everything we abhor, may be a risk. We need to choose carefully when, and how, to show love to the enemy. It is this type of love that can call the racist, the neo-Nazi, the KKK member, into another family—another way of living.

In showing love to people whom we would be inclined to hate—and who hate us—we may change that person's mind and behavior. Or maybe not. But at least we will know that we have acted in the way God would want us to act. And when we do that, we are being perfect—complete—as our heavenly Father is perfect.

SUING AND PURSUING YOUR NEIGHBOR

Readings:
1 Corinthians 6:1-11; Matthew 5:25-6

8

In fact, to have lawsuits at all with one another is already a defeat for you. Why not rather be wronged? Why not rather be defrauded? But you yourselves wrong and defraud—and believers at that.

1 Corinthians 6:7-8

We have already heard from Jesus about the importance of reconciling with a neighbor whom we think might be angry with us. But what happens when we *know* someone has a dispute with us? More, what if they seek to resolve that dispute in the way that so many disputes are resolved today—in a court of law?

In the first century, as in our own, both individuals and communities faced the practical question about what happens when disputes "in the family" arise. In the city of Corinth, some members of the fledgling assemblies gathered in Jesus's name were apparently suing each other in the local (pagan) courts. Paul condemns this practice, but not because he is against legal argument. Rather, he thinks there are better ways of resolving disputes than suing. "When any of you has a grievance against another," he asks, "do you dare to take it to court before the unrighteous"—here's that language of righteousness again—"instead of taking it before the saints?" (1 Corinthians 6:1).

The Greek *hagioi*, or holy ones, is usually translated into English as *saints*, and that is the term by which Paul refers to the people in these assemblies. They're all saints. "Do you not know that the saints will judge the world?" he writes in verse two. In other words: "You followers of Jesus, you're going to interact with the world at some point. Can't you settle with each other? And if you can't, you know what? The people on the outside will be even less impressed with you than they are already." He tells them, in essence, to get their act together: "If you have ordinary cases, then, do you appoint as judges those who have no standing in the church? I say to this to your shame" (vv. 4-5a).

Paul is not inventing a new doctrine. In the Sermon on the Mount, Jesus has already addressed the subject of lawsuits as part of his teaching on reconciliation. If someone sues you, Jesus says, "Come to terms quickly with your accuser while you're on the way to court with him, or your accuser may hand you over to the judge" (Matthew 5:25). If you take it to the courts, Jesus warns, all sorts of bad things might happen.

We're not talking here about Judge Judy. We're talking about courts where, particularly in pagan settings, judges bought their offices. We have evidence from later centuries of Christians going to Jewish courts because they figured they could get a fairer judgment than what they would find in their own courts.

What happens if, in fact, your neighbor's case against you is a strong one? Better reconcile now rather than let the court impose additional fees or fines on you—or you might even wind up in jail. Jesus uses an example of a financial debt. You owe your neighbor some money. Your neighbor will take you to court. You could be thrown into prison and won't get out until you've paid the last penny. The lesson: Pay the bill, or at least see if you can work things out with the family member (yes, we are still speaking about family and community) who holds the bond. Rather than sue a member of the family in the courts, "pur-sue" justice and reconciliation.

Today, as we see denominations splitting and people arguing about who has the right to the church property, or as we see denominations refuse funding for seminaries for particular reasons, Jesus's (and Paul's) teaching is more relevant than ever. If church is supposed to be a place where people come quickly to reconciliation with their opponents, where they practice forbearance and turn the other cheek, what kind of message does it send to the non-Christian when one Christian institution sues another? Or when someone who claims to be a Christian sues another member of the same church? That's precisely what Jesus doesn't want. Jesus wants these folks to be a lampstand that provide illumination for others—not a smudge.

THE GIFT
ON THE ALTAR

9

Readings:
Isaiah 58:1-12; Matthew 25:31-46

*Look, you serve your own interest on your fast day, and oppress all
your workers. Look, you fast only to quarrel and to fight and to strike
with a wicked fist. Such fasting as you do today will not make your
voice heard on high.*

Isaiah 58:3b-4

In his beginner's guide to the kingdom, Jesus gives a lesson
about proper worship. "So when you're offering your gift at the
altar," he begins—here he's referring to worship in the Jerusalem
Temple, but there may also be a hint of the story of Cain and Abel
in the background—"if you remember that your brother or sister has
something against you, leave your gift there before the altar and go;
first be reconciled to your brother or sister, and then come offer your
gift" (Matthew 5:23-24).

On a practical level, Jesus means that, if you want to engage in
any sort of religious practice, make sure that what is most important
gets taken care of first. In Judaism, what is more important is *always*
love of God and love of neighbor. So if you're screwing up on the love
of neighbor part, engage in some form of reconciliation before you
worship. The gift to God on the altar can wait.

Jesus is not talking about a grievance you may have against your
neighbor; he's talking about realizing that your neighbor has a grievance with you. This is the harder issue to recognize. We know when

we are annoyed, or worse, angry with another. We are sometimes oblivious, however, when we have created the hurt. Indeed, once we start thinking about how we may have hurt another, we become less likely to cause hurt.

We might ask ourselves, "Does it seem as if she is upset with me?" "Why hasn't he called?" "Could I have been overly critical, or not paid enough attention, or dismissed a major concern?" Then, Jesus tells us that we have to make the first move. Why? Because we can't fully worship God unless we've reconciled to those whom we have hurt, ignored, slighted, or dismissed. For Jesus and for Judaism, religion does not operate in a vacuum; we have to be in a connected (and therefore reconciled) community.

Jesus is also prioritizing the Torah and the Prophets, which consistently affirm that reconciliation is more important than sacrifice. That's what Hosea tells us: "For I desire steadfast love and not sacrifice" (6:6). Jesus will repeat that verse to the Pharisees and invite them to go study what it really means. It doesn't mean that sacrifice is unimportant. It means that mercy and reconciliation take priority.

Yom Kippur, Judaism's day of atonement, is about atoning, but it's also substantially and inseparably about reconciliation. According to Jewish custom, for the month before Yom Kippur, we seek out those we have hurt, or even think we have hurt, and we apologize and ask for forgiveness. We inventory our actions of the past year: where we came up short on sympathy or compassion; when we failed to extend a kind word and when we spoke in anger. Thus, when we come to reconcile with God, we have already reconciled with others.

Yom Kippur observance also involves a 25-hour fast. The *haftarah* reading (the reading from the Prophets) for that day comes from Isaiah 57 and 58—an admonition that proper fasting for repentance is not about starving one's body. God says, "Is not this the fast that

I choose: to loose the bonds of injustice, to undo the thongs of the yoke, to let the oppressed go free, and to break every yoke? Is it not to share your bread with the hungry, and bring the homeless poor into your house; when you see the naked, to cover them, and not to hide yourself from your own kin?" (Isiah 58:6-7). When your community worships in this way, God says, you will become like a flowing spring whose waters never fail. Your light will always shine. You will be called repairers of the breach and restorers of streets. *That* is a vision of the kingdom.

This passage resonates for me with what Jesus speaks in Matthew 25 about feeding the hungry and clothing the naked and seeing him in "the least of these"—people he calls his family. I also think this passage from Isaiah forms a marvelous intertext to Jesus's comment about offering your gift on the altar. Jesus and Isaiah are in harmony: True worship requires reconciliation; it requires loving the neighbor and the stranger, and acting upon that love.

RULES FOR CONFRONTATION

Readings:
Matthew 18:1-22; Ephesians 4:25-32;
2 Corinthians 2:5-10

10

"If another member of the church sins against you, go and point out the fault when the two of you are alone."

Matthew 18:15a

People will disagree; disagreeing is part of human nature, for we are not automatons who always think the same thoughts. At times, disagreement can be constructive. The rabbinic tradition speaks about "arguments for the sake of heaven" (*Pirke Avot* 5:17); that is, discussions worth having. To disagree and yet to retain respect for the person or party on the other side of the issue is not a sign of a broken fellowship. It is a sign of a healthy community.

But not all disagreements are healthy, and sometimes they can cause injury. When a member of the community sins against another member, the fellowship is broken. Complicating this issue, offenders sometimes do not realize the harm their words or actions created.

As with many communities, the broken relationship between individuals extends to the wider family as gossip, misinformation, and social pressure result in a nasty game of choosing sides. When one individual sins against another, that sin impacts more than just the two original parties. Unless that breach, that sin, is addressed by the congregation, it will spread like a virus until all are suffering. From such sin comes apostasy or schism, or worse.

In Matthew 18 (a great chapter, by the way), Jesus provides guidelines for addressing this situation. After telling the parable of the sheep that went astray and was returned to the fold, he begins, "So it is not the will of your Father in heaven that one of these little ones should be lost" (18:14). By invoking the "Father in heaven," he reminds his disciples not only of the "Our Father" prayer, but also of the new family gathered in his name. By speaking of these little ones, he attunes our ears to the "least of these" who need our help (Matthew 25:40, 45). To lose a member of the congregation would be like losing a member of the family. And yet, even within families, sin occurs, and sometimes the offender needs to be removed lest more damage occur.

Then come the instructions. Jesus begins by advising that if somebody in the community sins against another member, a disciple (by extension, a member of the clergy or a highly respected congregant) should have a chat with that person. No need for public shaming or a group intervention. That chat would be consistent with Leviticus 19:17-18, which teaches that reproving one's neighbor is part of loving one's neighbor.

The Epistle to the Ephesians (4:15, 25) offers a similar formula: Be angry, sure, but don't stew in your anger. Confront the offender, but say only what is useful for building up. Speak the truth in love, the author says, "for we are members of one another."

If after that meeting, the offending member repents and works to repair the effects of the sin, terrific. If not, Jesus advises, "take one or two others along with you, so that every word may be confirmed by the evidence of two or three witnesses" (Matthew 18:16). Otherwise put: send a committee and get the paperwork done. Sin cannot be allowed to go unattended.

If the committee does not succeed, the next move is to alert the entire congregation to the offense (18:17a). Social pressure is at work here, as the entire family seeks to bring the recalcitrant member back into the fold.

And if *that* doesn't work, Jesus advises, "Let such a one be to you as a Gentile and a tax collector" (18:17b). That is, the congregation removes the sinner from its fellowship. But the offender is *still* a part of the family. Baptism is indelible.

Why then "Gentile" and "tax collector?" Because it's precisely the Gentiles and the tax collectors to whom the mission is to go. Yes, sinners lose community privilege when they do not acknowledge their sin and do not work to repair the relationship. Yes, sometimes the hurt caused by the sin is too painful, too raw, to welcome the offender. Sometimes the sin remains a threat, and the congregation must protect itself. But the congregation, the family, does not give up on the sinner. The work of evangelization, of seeking those lost sheep, continues. The prodigal may yet return.

YOUR "YES" IS ENOUGH

Readings:
Judges 11:29-40; Matthew 5:33-7;
Matthew 23:16-24

11

When he saw her, he tore his clothes, and said, "Alas, my daughter! You have brought me very low; you have become the cause of great trouble to me. For I have opened my mouth to the Lord, and I cannot take back my vow."

Judges 11:35

In the last of the "extensions" in the Sermon on the Mount, Jesus states, "Again, you have heard that it was said to those of ancient times, 'You shall not swear falsely, but carry out the vows you have made to the Lord'" (Matthew 5:33); he then builds a fence around this law to protect it from being violated by insisting, "Do not swear at all" (Matthew 5:34).

Vows and oaths can be dreadful things. The concern for vows already surfaces in the Scriptures of Israel, in the story of Jephthah and his daughter (Judges 11). The story tells us that some vows should be broken. Indeed, some vows should never have been made in the first place.

During the time of the judges—a time when there was no king in Israel—the Israelite tribes were governed by a series of charismatic leaders. They were also facing a consistent downward slide from social order to chaos. As a child, Jepthah was driven from home by his half-siblings, but he grew to become a mighty warrior, and the Israelites in Gilead turned to him for military leadership.

Before a battle with the Ammonites, the spirit of the Lord comes upon Jephthah. But Jephthah—the tragic figure who doubts his own worth, the abused child who repeats what was done to him—makes a vow to God: "'If you will give the Ammonites into my hand, then whoever comes out of the doors of my house to meet me, when I return victorious from the Ammonites, shall be the LORD's, to be offered up by me as a burnt offering'" (Judges 11:30b-31).

He was not, contrary to popular belief, thinking of a dog wandering out of the house. If he were, that's already a horrible idea; dogs wouldn't be an appropriate burnt offering. He is thinking, although he does not give explicit voice to the thought, of his daughter, the most precious person in his house. He is bartering with God: I'll give you the person who is most precious to me, if you let me win. We can see the tragedy coming; we cannot stop it.

Victorious in battle, Jephthah returns. "Then Jephthah came to his home at Mizpah; and there was his daughter coming out to meet him with timbrels and with dancing. She was his only child; he had no son or daughter except her" (Judges 11:34). Seeing her, he mourns, "'For I have opened my mouth to the LORD, and I cannot take back my vow'" (Judges 11:35b). The rabbinic tradition condemns him; the Talmud quotes Jeremiah 8:22, "Is there no balm in Gilead? Is there no physician there?" (*Taanit* 4a).

The lesson is to not make rash vows to God as Jephthah did. Do not promise to God, "If you let me do X, then I will do Y." God doesn't need bribes.

Jesus then shifts the subject from vowing to swearing, and states, "Do not swear at all." He does not forbid certain vows, such as the Nazirite vow that Paul takes (see Acts 18:18). I doubt he'd have a problem with wedding vows (as long as people take them seriously). Rather, in regard to swearing, he is talking about the word we give to others.

Jesus forbids swearing by heaven (God's throne), by the earth (God's footstool), by Jerusalem (the city of the great king), even by one's head, "for you cannot make one hair white or black" (Matthew 5:36). (Actually, I have managed, in a nice and easy way, to make even more than one hair black, but now we're off the subject.) Jesus then makes his point: "Let your word be 'Yes, Yes' or 'No, No'" (Matthew 5:37a).

So what do we do? Ironically, people in courts or "swearing in" ceremonies who put their hands on Bibles and swear to tell the truth or uphold their commissions are swearing on a book that says, "Don't swear." Such swearing is meant to demonstrate honesty, sincerity, and commitment—but why should we have to swear that we are honest, sincere, or committed? What we say ultimately matters much less than what we do.

Hypocrisy annoys Jesus. He calls his followers to a higher righteousness, a righteousness manifested in deeds. I can picture him saying, "You don't have to swear that you will do something. If you say you'll do it, then we should all be able to trust you at your word. When you say yes, that ought to mean yes, and that ought to be enough."

PUBLIC DISPLAYS AND PRIVATE HOLINESS

12

Readings:
Matthew 6:1-5; Matthew 6:16-18

*"And whenever you fast, do not look dismal, like the hypocrites, for
they disfigure their faces so as to show others that they are fasting.
Truly I tell you, they have received their reward."*

Matthew 6:16

There are numerous reasons for attending church, synagogue, or
any worship service. If you go to church to be in fellowship with
others, terrific. If you find that worshiping with others reinvigorates
your relationship with God, superb. If you want to hear a word of
affirmation, comfort, challenge or inspiration; if you love to listen to
the choir; if the service reminds you of your happy days in Sunday
school or in youth groups and you rejoice when your children have
the same positive feelings, great.

But those who show up on Sunday morning with the agenda
of "Look at me, look at what a good Christian I am," then there's a
problem. The same point holds for Jews in the synagogue, Muslims
in the mosque, and even faculty at the convocation.

Jesus warns his disciples, repeatedly, against hypocrisy. The
word comes into English from the realm of ancient Greek theater,
where the *hypokrites* was an actor on stage. What the actor gives is a
performance, not an authentic life. Actors get applause for pretending
successfully to be other people. The disciple is not an actor; the
disciple seeks not accolades but a number of much more profound
concerns: community, reconciliation, compassion, peace, and love.

Hypocrites know who they are. But problems come about when people engaging in authentic religious expression get accused of hypocrisy. It may be the case that the sin of judgmentalism is more present in the congregation than hypocrisy. For example, in the worship service, opportunities for displaying piety take ever-new forms: arms waving in the air for prayer and song; arms outstretched for the Father; voices from the choir that soar above the others; swaying and clapping and stomping and shouting…My first impression with such expressions of worship was one of spectacle: I kept watching the performances, and so my focus was less on the worship and more on the worshipers. "What are you doing?" I wondered (to myself).

Then, figuring the question was worth asking, I approached a few of the more enthusiastic people in the congregation, all friends of mine, to ask about the outstretched hands and the waving arms. The answers I received made perfect sense. One young man told me, "I find that when I worship with my whole body—my arms and my voice, my hands and my feet—I better feel the presence of the Spirit." An older woman said, "I started singing loudly because this is my gift to God." Neither thought to "show off," and so I realized that I was at fault for judging. What I took for hypocritical displays instead flowed from honest motives.

Outside the church, common examples of public piety include the "meet at the flagpole" prayers in public schools and the professions of faith by politicians at prayer breakfasts. The flagpole approach to prayer, which is a legitimate exercise of freedom of religion, has the strong potential to fall into the category of "in order to be seen by others." God does not need cheerleaders and halfbacks setting up a praise band before the first bell. The practice of meeting at the flagpole has in some locations served less to glorify God than to marginalize those who practice a different type of religion, or no religion at all.

Let the high school students be aware that a practice that excludes others—that signals, "You are not at home in this community"—is not a practice that lets light shine. It would be good to know if those who sing hallelujah at the flagpole at 7 a.m. are showing love to others the rest of the day—especially when no one else is watching.

As for public professions of faith: I take Jesus at his word when he states, "Let your light shine before others, so that they may see your good works and give glory to your Father in heaven" (Matthew 5:16). If the prayers are not backed up by good works, they are empty words, heaped up for show. Such purveyors have already received their reward.

PRAYER:
IT'S PERSONAL

Reading:
Matthew 6:5-8

13

"But whenever you pray, go into your room and shut the door and
pray to your Father who is in secret...."

Matthew 6:6

As with other signs of piety, the difference between prayers that
Jesus commends and prayers he condemns concerns intent. For Jesus,
prayer is both about communicating with God and, at times, being
part of a community. It is not about performing for public approval on
a street corner or even saying words that will impress a congregation
during a worship service. For that reason, he says, go to your room
and shut the door when you're ready to talk with God about your own
concerns. Don't make it a show, and don't assume that God, who
already knows what you need, is going to be moved to action by fancy
words. As with most things of value, the issue is quality, not quantity.

Eight hundred or so years earlier, the prophet Joel made the same
point. He also understood the difference between sincere prayer and
showing off:

Yet even now, says the LORD,
        return to me with all your heart,
with fasting, with weeping, and with mourning;
        rend your hearts and not your clothing.

Toward the Kingdom of Heaven

Return to the LORD, your God,
       for he is gracious and merciful,
slow to anger, and abounding in steadfast love,
       and relents from punishing.

                                    Joel 2:12-13

Rending one's clothing was a sign that indicated grief or remorse; it also indicated mourning, as we might mourn over the lack of justice, the manifestations of hatred, or the complacency of those who have closed their eyes and ears to a suffering world. God calls for a deeper level of righteousness that is private: a rending of the heart.

Many of the Psalms (such as Psalm 22, which Jesus quotes from the cross) functioned, both in their origin and through the centuries, as personal prayers. Other personal prayers, ascribed to individuals, became increasingly prominent in the Second Temple period, the time of the return to Israel following the Babylonian exile in the sixth century BCE through the first century CE, the time of Jesus. In the book named after her, Judith issues a personal prayer, as does Esther in the Greek additions to her book. The book of Daniel has several additions of prayers, including the "Song of the Three Young Men." A Dead Sea Scroll known as 1QH (1 for the cave number; Q for Qumran; H for the Hebrew term *hodayot*, translated *thanks* or *thanksgiving*) contains the prayers most likely composed by the Teacher of Righteousness, the founder of the community. These prayers also serve as invitations to their readers: Esther, Judith, and Daniel pray; the Teacher of Righteousness at Qumran prays; therefore, you should pray too. You can pray the Psalms, you can adapt the words, you can say whatever you need to say. Be honest. Don't hold back. God is listening.

Jesus practices what he preaches. Occasionally, the Gospels record him offering a prayer in front of others, such as he makes just before raising his friend Lazarus from death (John 11:41b-42). And even here, he lets others know that the prayer is focused on God (the Father), not on him: "Father, I thank you for having heard me. I knew that you always hear me, but I have said this for the sake of the crowd standing here, so that they may believe that you sent me." Those opening comments are worth repeating. Just as Jesus is heard in prayer, so we are also heard in prayer. And when we do what God wants us to do—comfort the mourners, use our gifts in service to others—then those actions show that we are God's ambassadors.

More often, Jesus seeks a private place to pray. Luke 5:16 says Jesus does this frequently, especially as large crowds started following him. In the Gospel's next chapter, Luke tells us that before Jesus heals numerous people, he calls his disciples and teaches them how to pray: "during those days he went out to the mountain to pray; and he spent the night in prayer to God" (6:12). Jesus needed the time to pray—to speak with God, to express his feelings, to recharge through prayer—before he could commission, heal, and teach. Mark 1:34-35 tells us that after Jesus had "cured many who were sick with various diseases, and cast out many demons," that "in the morning, while it was still very dark, he got up and went out to a deserted place, and there he prayed." Even when he took some or all of the disciples with him, as in the story of the transfiguration (Luke 9) or on his final night on the Mount of Olives (Matthew 26), he separated himself from them when he prayed.

Jesus is *not* eliminating public prayer. He and his followers took part in synagogue worship, which involved communal prayers.

The Psalms are filled with prayers offered by the community and reflecting the community's concerns. What Jesus says to eliminate is the turning of prayer into a performance. Prayer should be a direct, heartfelt communication. When prayer is needed for solace, to recharge, or to express deep concerns, a large audience is not needed. Prayer can have an audience of one—the one God—and that is all the audience we need. A showy prayer does not improve the chances of getting the attention of the God of Israel, who already has heard the words of the heart.

RAISING MONEY WITHOUT RAISING EYEBROWS

Readings:
Matthew 6:2-4; Mark 12:41-44

14

"But when you give alms, do not let your left hand know what your right hand is doing."

Matthew 6:3

When Jesus criticizes people who have trumpets sound when they give to charity, he's engaging in a rhetorical flourish. While alms-giving was common, expected, and indeed required by the Torah, there is no evidence that fanfares were ever part of the routine. One made charitable donations because it was the right thing to do, not for the honor or the glory. Yet . . .

Fanfares of a sort do continue to sound. We inscribe names of benefactors on buildings; in the academy, we have named scholarships and named endowed chairs. Many of those names are those of the donors; others, such as several of the endowed chairs at Vanderbilt Divinity School, were created by funds collected by others to honor a particular individual. Do we give for our own name to be remembered or do we give so that the legacy of others will be recalled?

We see it at the symphony or a play when the program guide lists the donors and the amount of their donation. Worse, some of us are apt to judge: "They could have afforded more," or "How nice that they can be patrons of the arts—why aren't they giving to the local school system?" Better, Jesus says, to give in secret; don't even let your left hand know that your right hand has written the check. Perhaps with this teaching in mind, some benefactors insist on remaining anonymous. Or perhaps donations should more often be made in honor of others rather than to memorialize the self.

This dynamic also plays out in how congregations raise money. Several years ago, I took a group of Jewish youth in Nashville to a local church so they could experience Christian worship. Many things about the service surprised them. The first was the collection plate: "They're doing business on their Sabbath," one of our young people remarked. In the synagogue on the Sabbath, there is no collection since to handle money is to do business, or to give the impression of doing so. Jewish congregations have various ways of fundraising, but the collection plate on the Sabbath is not one of them.

The next thing that surprised the young people was the bringing of the offering to the altar: As the congregation stood and the music swelled, one of the younger children asked, "Are they worshiping the money?" "No," I told her. "It's a celebration of *tzekadah*." The term in Hebrew means *charity*, and it comes from the same root as the word for *righteousness*. That made sense to her.

Even so, I worry about the collection plate, and especially about churches that do not provide envelopes. Should the person on limited income who can only afford a dollar feel shamed when twenty-dollar bills sit in the plate? Should congregants be expected to write checks (so that no donation is anonymous, at least not to those who count the money and plan the budgets)? How does the idea of giving in secret comport with tax deductions for charitable donations?

And while we are contemplating these questions, how do we honor people like the impoverished widow whom Jesus observed donating two small copper coins, all the money she had or, as the Greek literally says, "her whole life" (Mark 12:41-44)? Do we understand charity primarily as a percentage of our income or do we only look at the bottom line? If the Gospel writers had given us the widow's name, perhaps it might be the next name inscribed on a building.

JESUS'S GUIDE
TO EYE CARE

15

Readings:
Matthew 6:22-23; Matthew 7:1-5; Matthew 23:1-3

"The eye is the lamp of the body. So, if your eye is healthy, your whole body will be full of light."

Matthew 6:22

Jesus's teaching in the Sermon on the Mount resounds with concern for hypocrisy—a concern John the Baptist addresses in Matthew 3 (although he skips the term "hypocrite" and goes straight to "brood of vipers" language) and that Jesus later develops in his invectives against the scribes and the Pharisees, people who were supposed to epitomize righteousness. When Jesus tells his disciples directly in Matthew 7:5, "'You hypocrite, first take the log out of your own eye, and then you will see clearly to take the speck out of your neighbor's eye,'" we learn that no group has a lock on hypocrisy. Jesus's harsh critiques (Matthew 23) of "scribes and Pharisees, hypocrites" are addressed also to Jesus's followers, and Matthew's readers, then and now. It would be, in a word, hypocritical to condemn others without first interrogating ourselves.

That self-check should precede any attempt to correct our neighbors, but correct we must. The famous statement from Leviticus 19:18b, "You shall love your neighbor as yourself: I am the LORD," is preceded by two statements about how we are to relate to our neighbor and, indeed, how we show love. The first part of that verse from Leviticus 19:18a reads, "You shall not take vengeance or bear a grudge against any of your people." We can see here the complement to Jesus's extension regarding the commandment against murder (Matthew 5:22). Jesus adds to "do not murder" the commandment "do not be angry." If one is not angry, one is less likely to murder. Leviticus says, "do not take vengeance," and then glosses, "do not [even] bear a grudge."

The immediately preceding verse in Leviticus 19:17 gets us to the question of how we must relate to our neighbors: "You shall not hate in your heart anyone of your kin; you shall reprove your neighbor, or you will incur guilt yourself." We take the log out of our own eye first by making sure that any reproof is based not in jealousy, pettiness, or hatred. And then we attempt to remove the speck. It is a sign of love to engage in helping through correction; it is a sign of hypocrisy when we correct in others the faults we allow to fester in ourselves.

In the community, our responsibility is to reprove our neighbors if we see them doing something wrong (Matthew 18). We don't let actions that are hurtful slide. To fail to stop a hurtful action is to aid and abet the perpetrator.

But reproof is not condemnation or damnation. Reproof is designed to restore community, not rend it asunder. The tradition of reproof is to call in, or call back, not to call out. And that practice must be done carefully.

When we see what is wrong, we don't shut our eyes. We try to restore the light. When we hear something bigoted, we don't close our ears. We try to offer a word of civility. At the same time, we do not hypocritically judge someone by impossible standards that we ourselves cannot meet. A single comment or action is not the sum total of an individual.

"'Do not judge, so that you may not be judged'" (Matthew 7:1) takes on additional meaning in the passion narrative, when Jesus is judged by a court, by the Sanhedrin, by Pilate, by the crowd, and even by the people today who read his story. And that gives a sense of our own responsibility for judging and its dangers. Judging is not merely saying something like, "Gosh, that suit is really unfortunate." It is also about condemning people to prison or to death. Judging is not an abstract issue. The Sermon on the Mount is not abstract. The Sermon on the Mount is about real-world concerns.

Teachings about hypocrisy and judging, teachings about how to respond to what we see and hear, also connect to our own personal health. Jesus says that, "if your eye is unhealthy, your whole body will be full of darkness" (Matthew 6:23a). Ophthalmologists have told me that the statement is medically true. It is also spiritually true. When we correct ourselves, and see sometimes how hard it is to stick to those corrections, we can reprove others with greater kindness and greater empathy. At that point, all logs and all specks are more easily removed.

RIGHTEOUSNESS RIGHTEOUSNESS, YOU SHALL PURSUE

16

Readings:
Psalm 99:1-5; Matthew 6:25-34; Philippians 4:10-13

"But strive first for the kingdom of God and his righteousness, and all these things will be given to you as well."

Matthew 6:33

At the end of chapter 6, Matthew devotes considerable attention to teachings about worries, faith, and trust. The worries concern basic needs: food, clothing, and shelter. Jesus's instruction, for some readers, may evoke images of Eden, where God provided everything for the humans of the garden as well as for the birds of the air and the lilies of the field. There might be a subtle reminder here, too, of Israel's history, when God provided food and water to sustain the people for forty years in the wilderness—with enough on the sixth day so that the people did not have to worry about gathering food on the sabbath. God had it covered. We hear in these recollections Jesus's portrayal of God as a loving Father who protects and provides for God's children.

Near the end of his call to trust, Jesus includes also a call to right conduct, to "strive first for the kingdom of God and his righteousness" (Matthew 6:33). If you're doing the right thing, Jesus says, then don't worry about tomorrow because you can't do anything about it anyway. Take care of today's concerns. The Father who got you through today, and all the days before that, knows what you need and will get you through tomorrow as well. The disciples can rest assured because they know that others in their group, their mother and brothers and sisters, are there to help them.

In prison, Paul writes to the Philippian community he founded. He can rejoice because he knows that the community has remained faithful; he rejoices because he has learned to be content with the little he has. Like a Stoic, Paul has determined what is needed and what is not. If we get rid of the clutter, we are better able to strive for righteousness; if we triage our worries, we are better able to get through the day; if we have firm foundation based on those treasures laid up in heaven (I may have just mixed a metaphor), we'll do just fine.

When we know what is important, then we can strive for righteousness. The quote echoes Deuteronomy 16:20a, but we would not know it because of the English translation. Deuteronomy reads, "Justice, and only justice, you shall pursue." The Hebrew for *justice* is *tzedek*, a cognate of the terms translated *righteousness*, *support for the poor,* and even *saintliness*. In the Septuagint, the Greek translation of this Hebrew text, *tzedek* becomes *dikaios*, a cognate of the term in Matthew 6:33, *dikaiosynē*. There can be no righteousness without justice; there can be no justice without care for the poor. And there can be no saintliness when our words and our actions do not promote these values.

Why are we to "pursue justice" or "strive for his righteousness?" Why not just say "be just" and "be righteous?" Those imperatives tell us that we do not need to get to perfect justice or perfect righteousness. We don't have to worry about not achieving all of our goals. Only God offers true and complete justice and righteousness. Our task is to pursue, to strive, to do the best we can. Upshot: stop worrying and start acting. At the end of the day, we'll feel better.

LIGHT AND BLINDNESS

17

Readings:
Matthew 6:22-23; Matthew 7:3-5;
Matthew 23:13-25

"Let them alone; they are blind guides of the blind. And if one blind person guides another, both will fall into a pit."

Matthew 15:14

I have never appreciated using the language of disability when it serves as a metaphor for evil actions or intent, although such metaphors are endemic to the English language. "That was a lame argument"; "Her comments fell on deaf ears"; "The umpire was surely blind"; "What a retarded comment." When I was a child, I recall hearing Helen Keller jokes (which I shall not repeat and you should not look up). We need better language to express our opinions.

Leviticus 19, the chapter that gives the commandments to love God and to love the neighbor, also mandates, "You shall not revile the deaf or put a stumbling block before the blind; you shall fear your God: I am the LORD" (v. 14). Deuteronomy 27:18a adds, "'Cursed be anyone who misleads a blind person on the road.'" Job testifies to his own care for the blind,

> because I delivered the poor who cried,
> and the orphan who had no helper.
> The blessing of the wretched came upon me,
> and I caused the widow's heart to sing for joy.
> I put on righteousness, and it clothed me;
> my justice was like a robe and a turban.

Light and Blindness

I was eyes to the blind,
and feet to the lame.
I was a father to the needy,
and I championed the cause of the stranger.
                                    Job 29:12-16

We can take these good biblical prompts, extend them (or build a fence around them to protect them), and do more. Here are three steps we can take.

First, despite the good intentions of these passages, we must eradicate the idea that blind people are helpless and hopeless, tragic victims whose lives are entirely dependent on the charity of others. And so those of us who are sighted will think that two blind people walking together will surely stumble. That would be the wrong impression. Blind people adapt to their condition; they do not get lost; they do not fall into pits. In blackouts, they are better able to navigate than the sighted; their other senses are heightened.

Second, we need to rid ourselves of other negative stereotypes that sometimes accompany descriptions of those who cannot see, hear, or walk. For example, some of my New Testament students believe that Jews did not allow the blind (or anyone else with a physical handicap) into the Jerusalem Temple because they were ritually impure. Wrong: none of these conditions is related to impurity. Indeed, Matthew's Gospel shows the error of that view when it reports, "The blind and the lame came to him in the Temple, and he cured them" (21:14).

Third, we do well to see Jesus as a man of his time. He uses the language of blindness to talk about those who disagree with his teachings. Such idioms were part of his culture and part of the broader Gentile world as well. But that was then, and now our ears should be more attuned to the impact our words can have. We are better off using his other language related to sight: of taking the logs out of our eyes; of being the light of the world; of making sure that we do not look with lust; of doing the right thing for the right reasons, and not because we want to be "seen by others"; and of avoiding giving someone the "evil eye," that is, of looking at them with malicious intent.

OUR FATHER

"Pray then in this way...."
Matthew 6:9a

Matthew's version of the "Our Father" prayer contains an orderly six petitions, which makes it easy to remember. The prayer is both vertical (the relationship between the individual and God) and horizonal (how we relate to other people); otherwise put, it is cruciform. Thus, it connects to what Jesus identifies as the greatest commandment (Matthew 22:36-40): love of God (Deuteronomy 6:5) and love of neighbor (Leviticus 19:18). Even the first two words of the prayer indicate this relationship: "Our" points to the horizontal, to the community; "Father" points to the vertical, to God.

Jesus was asked about the greatest commandment, but he answered with two commandments. In his view, belief should lead to right action: if we have love for God, we would want to do what God wants us to do. Yet even if we do not have a strong theological orientation—for belief is more a gift and a calling than a choice—we can still control our actions. If the actions in turn lead to belief in God, or even if they make us more aware of how interconnected our lives are, of how we really are our brother's [and sister's] keeper (see Genesis 4), then the actions will have benefited us as well as those who receive them.

We can always pray—in the car; in the shower; in the evening quiet. I suspect my students do a fair amount of praying in the classroom, especially before exams or oral presentations. Prayers prayed in a community have a different impact. In Jewish practice, certain prayers must be said with a *quorum* of ten Jewish adults called the *minyan*. Why ten? Not surprisingly, the tradition gives multiple answers. It could be that when Abraham argued with God over the fate of Sodom, the argument ended with a quorum of ten: "Then [Abraham] said, 'Oh do not let the Lord be angry if I speak just once more. Suppose ten are found there.' [God] answered, 'For the sake of ten I will not destroy it'" (Genesis 18:32). Or ten men form the smallest unit for the people in the wilderness generation: "Moses chose able men from all Israel and appointed them as heads over the people, as officers over thousands, hundreds, fifties, and tens" (Exodus 18:25). Or in the book of Ruth (4:2), Boaz gathers ten men to serve as witnesses to him arranging his marriage to Ruth.

Whatever the explanation, the *minyan* means that, along with private and personal prayers, Jews pray as part of a community. Jesus speaks of his presence "where two or three are gathered in [his] name" (Matthew 18:20) and his comment evokes the same idea. To pray "Our Father" is to be part of community; to show love of neighbor, one must have a neighbor to show that love, and from whom to receive that love. Indeed, after creating a world that was "very good," God then realizes something in this creation is "not good": "Then the LORD God said, 'It is not good that the man should be alone'" (Genesis 2:18a). To call God "Our Father" is therefore, necessary, to remind ourselves of other people in the family, who claim the same Father.

The address to God of "Father" was already known in Judaism by Jesus's time, and it likely became a hallmark of Jesus's teaching. His followers found in it a way of speaking of their own relationship to God and of recalling Jesus's intimate relationship to his divine

Father. "Father" language actually increases as we move from Mark, the earliest Gospel, to Matthew to Luke and finally to John. Perhaps as the congregations which gathered in his name became more and more ethnically diverse, "Father" language helped them find their commonality and so unity.

There's a Western Christian tradition known as *Lectio Divina* (Latin for *divine reading*). Read a text or just a verse; then reflect on the images it creates in your mind, meditate on it, and contemplate what it might mean for you. Take each word of the prayer: Our, Father, Name, Bread, Debt, Test... Each term leads to new associations, new devotions, and ideally, new questions as we seek its connotations in the biblical text, in our own lives, and in our communities.

THE POLITICS OF PRAYER

19

Readings:
Matthew 6:9; John 18:33-38

Jesus answered, "My kingdom is not from this world."
John 18:36a

There are several things worth considering when saying, "Our Father which art in heaven..." Here are two.

First, the Shakespearean-sounding "which art" (Matthew 6:9 KJV) has the romanticism of transporting us back to the early seventeenth century when the King James Version of the Bible was first printed. Even in churches where the vernacular is ordinarily used, somehow this prayer retains the "art" rather than "are" and "thy" rather than "your" language. There's an appeal in the thees and thous; the language not only connects us across time to the classic translation; it also seems to bridge the divide between heaven and earth. If we are to speak with God, perhaps we need special language, language that sounds formal.

Yet for the people who first prayed the King James Version of the "Our Father," there was nothing distinct about the language. "Thee" and "thou" were part of the vernacular. People in early seventeenth-century England were not being formal with the language of their prayer any more than Latin speakers who prayed in Latin, or Aramaic speakers who prayed the original "Our Father." We who pray to God today do not need this formality either, any more than we need to say to our dinner guests, "Wouldst thou pass the butter?" We do not need special or formal language to talk to God any more than we need special or formal language to talk with a loving parent.

Second, and more important, "Our Father in heaven" was (and remains) a political statement. The Roman Emperor Augustus, who was ruling at the time of Jesus's birth, was called *pater patriae*—father of the Fatherland—much as we style George Washington as the father of this country. Augustus, by the way, also called himself the son of God, since his adopted father, Julius Caesar, was formally deified by the Roman Senate. To pray "Our Father in heaven" and then to add, "your kingdom come" can be nothing other than a political wish: the ruler we have is not the one we need, and the kingdom we have is not the one we want.

To pray to "Our Father in heaven" means that our father, our ruler, our benefactor, our savior is *not* the one sitting on the empire's throne. When in the Gospel of John, Jesus tells Pilate, "My kingdom is not from this world" (18:36), he is on the one hand assuring the governor that he is not a political threat, that he is not engaged in an armed revolutionary struggle. But he is, on the other hand, saying that his way is not the way the world works. His kingdom is one of peace, not military might; it is one where everyone is recognized as being in the image and likeness of God, not just the emperor and his retinue. His is one where followers pursue justice, wherever that pursuit might lead.

In the synagogue, after the congregation recites the *Shema* ("Hear, O Israel: the LORD is our God, the LORD alone" [Deuteronomy 6:4]), it recites silently a second verse. Originally, the verse served as a type of "amen" to the *Shema*: "Blessed be his glorious name forever" (from Psalm 72:19). After the destruction of the Jerusalem Temple in 70 CE by the Romans, that second verse became modified, and this new version is recited to this day: "Blessed be the name of his glorious kingdom for ever and ever." The inclusion of "kingdom" language reinforces the fact that God's kingdom is not Rome's empire. The inclusion of "for ever and ever" speaks not only for this world, but also for the world to come.

By teaching his disciples to pray "Your kingdom come," Jesus reminds them, and us, that our allegiance is to a kingdom, and a king, other than the Roman Empire and its emperor—or any other state that is based on military coercion, racism, sexism, antisemitism, or the plethora of human sins that fail to recognize that we are all in the divine image and should be treated with love.

WHO'S YOUR ABBA?

Readings:
Micah 7:1-9; Malachi 4:5-6;
Matthew 10:21-22, 32-39; Matthew 8:18-22

20

Whoever loves father or mother more than me is not worthy of me...."
Matthew 10:37a

In Matthew's mission discourse (chapter 10), just a few chapters after the Sermon on the Mount, Jesus says, "Do not think that I have come to bring peace to the earth; I have not come to bring peace, but a sword. For I have come to set a man against his father, and a daughter against her mother" (vv. 34-35a). We saw him do just that right before the Sermon on the Mount, when he called James and John to be his disciples while they're with their father, Zebedee, in their fishing boat. They leave their father and follow Jesus. If Zebedee ever registered an opinion about his sons walking away from the family business, Matthew does not share it with us. Perhaps Mrs. Zebedee, who joins her sons in following Jesus, encouraged her husband to travel with them.

Jesus is not original in his statement. The eighth century BCE prophet Micah issued a similar warning about the breakdown of the family: "The son treats the father with contempt, the daughter rises up against her mother, the daughter-in-law against her mother-in-law; your enemies are members of your own household" (Micah 7:6).

In Matthew 23, Jesus says, "And call no one your father on earth, for you have one Father—the one in heaven" (v. 9). He is establishing priorities: loyalty to and service to God come before any marital or biological relationship.

When a disciple asks Jesus, "Lord, first let me go and bury my father" (Matthew 8:21) before crossing the Sea of Galilee, Jesus refuses his request. We should not imagine that the man's father has just died; if he had, the disciple would be at the burial with his family. In all likelihood, the disciple is talking about what is known as "secondary burial," a practice well-attested among Jews in the late Second Temple period.

After a corpse had been entombed for a year, family members would collect the bones and put them in bone boxes called *ossuaries*. Frequently, the bones of family members would be placed in the same box. Numerous ossuaries have been preserved, including that of Caiaphas the high priest. Whether the ossuary with the inscription: "Jacob, son of Joseph, brother of Jesus" is that of James (the so-called "James ossuary") is a forgery, or whether it belongs to *the* James known from Acts 15, Josephus's *Antiquities*, and select New Testament epistles, remains debated.

Jesus's disciple is not asking to attend the funeral, but he may be asking for a delay of almost a year. To that, Jesus says no. The call of discipleship, and of the new family the disciples represent, is more urgent.

These stories and sayings are difficult, because in some cases the message of the prophet or the call of Jesus did separate families. Aside from interreligious marriages—which is not what either Micah or Jesus was considering—we see families disintegrating over political views or economic policies. And in many of these cases, the Bible becomes weaponized in the arguments over such topics as immigration, healthcare, resource allocation, gun rights, abortion, and so on. Such separation is not a good thing; it is, however, reality. The biblical text tells us that enmity in the family happens. No one is blamed; everyone is involved; reconciliation is possible.

Toward reconciliation, the Bible gives us resources. For Jesus, and for his Jewish tradition, since God is our Father, we are all children of God. To call God *abba*, Father, is not to address God as if we are toddlers—for despite the popular view, *abba* does not mean "daddy" or "papa" (and nor is one to pray to the Swedish band that gave us *Mamma Mia!*). Rather, those who call God "Father" are children of all ages who recognize the role the Father had in shaping their lives, in protecting them, and of being the source of wisdom, comfort, and support. It is belief in this Father who in some cases can hold the family together; in other cases, this Father supports us when the arguments become too volatile. If we can no longer be in relationship with our biological or adoptive fathers, we still have the Father in heaven.

Finally (literally), the last verse of the Old Testament (that is, in the Christian canonical order) is Malachi 4:6, God's promise sent to the prophet Elijah, to "turn the hearts of parents to their children and the hearts of children to their parents, so that I will not come and strike the land with a curse." The divine desire is not to punish because families have come to hate each other; the divine will is for reconciliation of all God's children.

MAKING GOD'S NAME HOLY

21

Readings:
Matthew 6:9; Ezekiel 36:16-36

I will sanctify my great name ... and the nations shall know that I am the LORD, says the Lord GOD, when through you I display my holiness before their eyes.

Ezekiel 36:23

In Judaism, there's a well-known prayer called the *Kaddish*; the name comes from the Hebrew root *k-d-sh*, which means *holy*. The prayer has different versions, and these different versions are recited at different times in the liturgy. Its best-known version, called the "Mourner's Kaddish," is recited for eleven months by people whose close family members have died, and then again every year on the anniversary (*yahrzeit*, a Yiddish term, literally, *year-time*) of the loved one's death. The name of the dead community member is read aloud in the synagogue; traditionally, a small light next to a memorial plaque bearing the name of the deceased is lit; the family at home will light a memorial candle. The name of the deceased is recalled, and with the recollection of the name comes the recollection of the memories.

As with certain other prayers, the Kaddish should be recited with a *minyan*, a quorum of ten. One should not mourn alone, and in Jewish practice, the community is always present to be with the mourner. That quorum demonstrates that the community continues, and the community along with the family members thereby honors the memory of the dead.

The prayer, which praises the name of the divine, says nothing about death. It begins rather with the insistence that God's name be magnified and sanctified. Jesus, too, invokes the holiness of God's name in the prayer that he teaches. "Hallowed be your name" or "hallow-ed be thy name" (Matthew 6:9) is not an empty verse between the more important "Our Father" and "Your kingdom come." Yet I find people skip over this hallowing quickly. That may be because we do not take names as seriously as we might, and we do not always take the time to consider what it means to "hallow" anything, let alone a name.

What does it mean to make a name holy? When we act in a way that reflects our self-understanding that we are children of God, when we have internalized the *mitzvot*, the commandments, and have built those appropriate fences around them, then we honor the name of our Father by our actions. More, we honor the Father's name when we personally find the peace that comes with doing the will of the Father.

The prophet Ezekiel, writing during the Babylonian exile in the sixth century BCE, speaks of how some of the people dishonored the divine name, whether by infidelity to their community, by sinning, or by blaspheming. Such reactions would not be surprising: having witnessed the destruction of their Temple, having been forced-marched from the conquered Jerusalem to what is now Iraq, many of the people may well have acted out of their devastation. Yet the majority prevailed; they remained faithful to the covenants that God established with their ancestors and with Moses, and they knew that God remained faithful to them. In exile, without sacred space, they kept the sacred time of the Sabbath. In exile, without the Temple or the Davidic king, they began to put together the Torah in the form we still have it today. In exile, they remembered the songs of Zion and they sang them to their children.

They did as Deuteronomy 6:7-9 commands: "Recite [the words of the Torah] to your children and talk about them when you are at home and when you are away, when you lie down and when you rise. Bind them as a sign on your hand, fix them as an emblem on your forehead, and write them on the doorposts of your house and on your gates." The sign and emblem on the hand and forehead are the phylacteries (or in Hebrew, *tefillin*) Jesus mentions in Matthew 23:5; on the doors of Jewish households to this day one finds a *mezuzah* (Hebrew: *doorpost*), a small case containing the parchment (or sometimes now paper) on which is written Deuteronomy 6:4-9; 11:13-21. All these practices serve to sanctify, to make holy, the divine name.

With their bad conduct and their idol worship in Babylon, the people have profaned God's name among the nations. And yet, God declares, for the sake of that holy name, God will return the exiles to their own land and put a new spirit within them; then the land that had been desolate will become like the Garden of Eden. Even when we despair, God is present with us. And when God's name is treated by the people as holy, the sanctifying effects extend to the whole community.

By proclaiming that he has not come to abolish the Torah but to fulfill it, Jesus is sanctifying the divine name. By building a fence about the Law to make sure that his followers follow the *mitzvot* and do more than what the written text requires, he is making sacred God's name. By following his teachings, his disciples already are making sure that the divine name is hallowed. And by remembering the people who are no longer with us in body, we hallow their names as well.

YOUR WILL BE DONE: WHAT WE MUST DO

Readings:
Matthew 6:10; Micah 6:6-8; Luke 16:19-31

"Your kingdom come. Your will be done, on earth as it is in heaven."

Matthew 6:10

Matthew often talks about the kingdom of heaven rather than the kingdom of God. For Matthew, heaven is a real place, up there, where God is—a place where God's will is always done. The idea of the kingdom of heaven runs right through the Sermon on the Mount. And so does the connection between "your kingdom come" and "your will be done."

When God's will is being done, that is, by us, then that kingdom is in some sense already present. When we realize that since "God saw everything that he had made, and indeed, it was very good" (Genesis 1:31), we should treat the heavens and the earth and all that is in them, all that God made, with respect, then the kingdom is present. When we realize that we all bear the divine image —"So God created humankind in his image, in the image of God he created them; male and female he created them" (Genesis 1:27)—that we are all part of the same family, no matter how we look, pray, or love, then the kingdom is present. The veil between the "up there" and the "down here" becomes lifted. As Tobit advises his son, "Give alms from your possessions, and do not let your eye begrudge the gift when you make it. Do not turn your face away from anyone who is poor, and the face of God will not be turned away from you" (Tobit 4:7).

At the end of the Sermon on the Mount, Jesus says, "Not everyone who says to me, 'Lord, Lord' will enter the kingdom of heaven, but only the one who does the will of my Father in heaven" (Matthew 7:21). Jesus, as Matthew shows, links the kingdom to a concern for doing what needs to be done. In other words, get out there and do God's will. To recite the "Our Father" while ignoring the extensions that come before it (for example, don't be angry, love your enemy), then we're missing the point of the prayer. It would be hypocrisy—something that Jesus really can't stand—to say to God, "Your will be done," and then not do it ourselves.

If "Your will be done" is partly our responsibility, then the obvious question becomes: How do you do God's will? And the answer is equally obvious: God has already conveyed God's will through the Torah and through its ongoing interpretation. That is why in Jesus's parable about the rich man and poor Lazarus, when the rich man asks Father Abraham to send Lazarus back to warn his five brothers of the consequences of ignoring his neighbor in need, Abraham replies: "'They have Moses and the prophets; they should listen to them'" (Luke 16:29). Listen, discuss, and then, for heaven's sake, fulfill it.

According to *Pirke Avot*, Rabban Gamliel, the son of Judah the Prince (who codified the Mishnah ca. 200 CE), said both "all learning of Torah which is not joined with labor is destined to be null and cause sin" and "all who work with the community—let them work with them for the sake of heaven" (*Pirke Avot* 2.2). To study the texts and not follow through by doing what they command is to stop short.

Jesus says, "Not one stroke of the Torah will pass away" (Matthew 5:18, my paraphrase), so go learn it, learn how it has been interpreted over time, question it, and then act on what you have learned. By asking, "Your will be done," what we're saying in effect is: "Give us the strength, give us the courage, give us the opportunity, in order to do your will."

PRAY BOLDLY

Let us therefore approach the throne of grace with boldness....

Hebrews 4:16

Imperatives are commands, and most of us do not want to be on the receiving end of them. Our resistance starts early: "Clean your room" and "Do your homework" are not often met with a "Happily, Mom" or "Right away, Dad." Resistance (albeit unspoken) may continue for those who serve in the military: "Attention, Right Face, Forward March, Double Time..." There are employers who demand, "Get this done by closing time"; there are even professors who demand, "Use good grammar" (although I know for a fact this command does not get much traction).

God speaks to us in the imperative often. To Abraham, God commands, "'Go from your country and your kindred and your father's house to the land that I will show you'" (Genesis 12:1). That "go" is in the imperative; God's words are not a request, but a demand. When God commands, "Honor your father and your mother" (Exodus 20:12), this is not request but a mandate.

Ironically, magnificently, many Jewish prayers use the imperative with God. The famous Psalm 22, which underlies much of Matthew's crucifixion account, calls to God in the imperative, "Save me from the mouth of the lion!" (Psalm 22:21). This is not a request; it is an agonizing demand. In less desperate circumstances,

Psalm 25:4-5a demands, "*Make* me to know your ways, O LORD; *teach* me your paths. *Lead* me in your truth, and *teach* me, for you are the God of my salvation" (italics added).

The "Our Father" carries over this tradition. "Hallowed be your name" is an imperative (for those who like grammar, it is technically a third singular aorist passive imperative). It is saying to God and to others as well: "Make that divine name holy." As for that heavenly kingdom: Make it happen! Make your will be done! Give us the bread, both to sustain our bodies and to be eaten in that messianic banquet! To use the imperative with God is sometimes known as approaching God with boldness. Say what is on your heart, and demand—yes, demand—"Shall not the Judge of all the earth do what is just?" Those are not my words; this is what Abraham said to God upon God's decision to wipe out the people of Sodom (Genesis 18:25).

There's a nice line in the Epistle to the Hebrews: "Let us therefore approach the throne of grace with boldness so that we may receive mercy and find grace to help in time of need" (4:16). 1 John teaches about speaking boldly before God several times (3:21; 4:17; 5:14), for if God is love (1 John 4:8) and we are to love God with all our hearts (Deuteronomy 6:5, a quote Jesus repeats), then our relationship is a mutual one of boldness—of forthrightness, of demanding what is right. In other words, tell God what you want, be bold about it, and don't hold back. God knows what is in our hearts anyway, so we might as well give those feelings voice. Once voiced, we can better deal with them.

Even though the "Our Father" is directed to God, the imperative to hallow is partly our responsibility. Making holy also means to be set apart; making something holy means moving it from the realm of the profane, the ordinary, the quotidian to the realm of the holy, the special, the sanctified. There's nothing wrong with the profane— that is, the ordinary and the everyday. Things, places, and people become holy when we recognize their sanctity. A table can be a profane object, but when people are seated around it, sharing food and fellowship, showing love of God and of neighbor, that table becomes sacred, hallowed.

The word *God* is just a word; by spelling it with a capital G, we move toward signaling the holiness of the name. But it only becomes hallowed when, with the strength and courage God gives us, we act in such a way that we feel the power, and others see the light. In hallowing the divine name, God sanctifies us even as we, ironically, sanctify God. The book of Acts consistently speaks of how the followers of Jesus proclaim their faith "boldly" (9:27-28; 13:46; 14:3; 18:26; 19:8); Paul's letters, substituting for the apostle himself, are bold reminders (Romans 15:15; Ephesians 6:20) of his faith and the faith of the recipients.

Paul refers to everyone in the assemblies he addresses as "saints;" the Greek term is *hagioi*, which is where we get the term *hagiography*, the biography of a saint. It really means *holy ones*. They are saints, even when his letters make clear that they have behaved in ways that were anything but saintly. They are saints on their way. They are marching in, but they've not yet arrived. Go boldly and demand what is right.

BREAD FROM THE EARTH, BREAD FROM HEAVEN

Readings:
Isaiah 25:6-10; Matthew 6:11; 1 Corinthians 3:5-9

24

"Give us this day our daily bread."
Matthew 6:11

The prayer, "Give us this day our daily bread" is not only redundant, but it is also odd. If we translate the Greek along the lines of "give us tomorrow's bread today" and think about the desire for that eschatological banquet, where we all recline at table with Abraham, Isaac, and Jacob, our parents and our grandparents, and all the loved ones who are no longer present with us in the flesh, then the prayer works well. But if we say, "Give us this day our daily bread," not only are we being redundant, we are also missing a few steps.

God does not give us bread, fully baked and ready to eat. If we are thinking of daily sustenance, we might pray, "Give us this day healthy seed, fertile soil, and sufficient rain and sunshine." And while you're at it, "Give us this day wise farmers, skilled harvesters, strong millers, and patient bakers." Someone has to plant the seeds, tend the field, harvest the grain, mill it, create dough, and do the baking before the bread is placed on the table or on the tongue.

This line of the "Our Father," as it is traditionally recited, reminds me of the Jewish prayer said before meals in which bread products are served: "Blessed are you, Lord our God, ruler of the universe, who brings forth bread from the earth." The prayer is called the *motzi*, from the Hebrew for "who brings forth." Again, the prayer asks us to fill in a few steps.

Bread from the Earth, Bread from Heaven

The rabbis understood the process, and the difficulties, involved in cultivating grain and making bread. They were always mindful, as we should be, of those who did the farming, the harvesting, the kneading, and the baking. There are *mitzvot* (commandments) to help with the entire process, just as today's farmers and bakers have best practice models. Some Christian mealtime prayers make a similar acknowledgment when they ask God to bless not only the meal but the hands that prepared it. (As I write this, while people are sheltering in their homes and socially distanced amid a pandemic, we have belatedly come to recognize those who prepare food, those who deliver it, and those who stock the shelves of our stores as "essential workers.")

For Israel, for Jesus, and for Paul, the bringing forth of bread is a team effort: people in the community working together, and all working under the authority and under the love of God. Paul addresses both the work of humans and the ultimate sovereignty of God—and the life of the community, too—when he calls the contentious believers in Corinth "God's field." Servants like Paul had planted the seeds, others like Apollos the preacher had watered the field, but it was God who brought about the growth. It turns out that when it comes to daily bread, of the literal as well as the metaphorical varieties, we all have essential roles to play.

Rabbi Nehemiah, who lived in the century after Jesus, argued that the *motzi* was actually about this future time when God would restore God's created order, and bread would not require human toil but only human trust. In asking for tomorrow's bread, Jesus is extending the request that God's kingdom come and God's will be done: Today, Lord, bring about the day when you "will destroy on this mountain the shroud that is cast over all peoples"; when you "will swallow up death forever"; and when you "will wipe away the tears from all faces" (Isaiah 25:7-8).

I think we need both of these prayers—the one acknowledging our dependence on God in the present age, the other anticipating God's perfect justice in the age to come. We also need to reflect on what it means to speak about "bread" and not consider the process, and the people, who produce it. To bake bread in our own kitchens can be a joy; for others, to bake bread is a chosen career. For still others—those who harvest the grain, mill it, and package the bread in factories, it is a difficult, exhausting job. The next time you hold a piece of bread in your hand, give thanks, for all.

FORGIVE US OUR DEBTS?

25

Readings:
Matthew 6:12-14; Leviticus 25:35-38;
Matthew 18:23-35; Deuteronomy 15:7-11

"And out of pity for him, the lord of that slave released him and forgave him the debt."

Matthew 18:27

Many Christians learn Jesus's prayer the way I did in elementary school with the verse, "Forgive us our trespasses." We may not have known what trespasses were; I thought that walking on the grass by the library with its "do not trespass" sign was something that we shouldn't do, but if we did, we would be forgiven by God if we asked. But in Matthew's Gospel, the "Our Father" prayer uses the language of debts. While in Aramaic and Hebrew, "debt" is another way of speaking about sin (we can see how this metaphor functions in English when we speak of "forgiving a debt" or "forgiving a loan"), we can't escape the economic implications of "forgive us our debts." Jesus wanted his disciples not only to forgive the sins that they committed against each other; he also wanted them to live in an economically just way.

That sense of economic justice was already part of his Jewish heritage, as we see even in the Hebrew language, where the word for *charity, tzedakah,* is from the same root as the word for *righteousness, tzedek.* Deuteronomy 15:11 mandates, "Since there will never cease to be some in need on the earth, I therefore command you, 'Open your hand to the poor and needy neighbor in your land.'" Similarly, Deuteronomy 24:14 instructs, "You shall not withhold the wages of poor and needy laborers, whether other Israelites or aliens who reside in your land in one of your towns." The prophets continually advocate for the poor, and Proverbs 31:9 insists, "Speak out, judge righteously, defend the rights of the poor and needy."

Just as Jesus builds a fence around the commandment against murder by forbidding anger, and just as he builds a fence around the commandment against adultery by forbidding lust, so we might see him building a fence about the commandments regarding debts by insisting that all debts within his group be forgiven.

The Torah forbids the charging of interest to fellow Jews. Exodus 22:25 reads, "If you lend money to my people, to the poor among you, you shall not deal with them as a creditor; you shall not exact interest from them;" and twice more in Leviticus 25:35-38 and Deuteronomy 23:20, the commandment is repeated. Charging interest to foreigners is allowed. Many of my students condemn such a practice as ethnocentric, if not xenophobic. I don't agree with them. We might think of our own tariff laws, which impose fees on certain goods imported from outside the United States but not on the same, competing goods produced domestically. Or, for another example, parents might give interest-free loans to their children, but it is less likely that they will be as generous to strangers. The notion that Israelites were loaning funds to non-Israelites shows precisely that they are not xenophobic; if they were, they would not be engaged in mutual economic activities.

Perhaps building a fence around this law, Jesus simply forbids holding a debt. He is not talking to strangers; he is talking to his disciples—whom he regards as his family, members of the same community. That is the idea underlying Deuteronomy 15:7: "If there is among you anyone in need, a member of your community in any of your towns within the land that the LORD your God is giving you, do not be hard-hearted or tight-fisted toward your needy neighbor." The translation is not quite right; the Hebrew translated "a member of your community" is literally "your brother." Community members are family, and in families, generosity is expected when a member falls on hard times.

As we have seen, Jesus redefines the family in terms of doing the Father's will as he understands it. In this new family, not only are sins forgiven, but also debts are forgiven. Jesus tells a parable in Matthew 18:23-35 about a slave who owed his master, a king, the astronomical sum of 10,000 talents. Because the slave cannot repay the debt, the king plans on selling him, his wife, and children in order to recoup at least some of those talents. The slave begs for mercy, and the king, magnanimously, wipes out the debt. But then this same slave encounters a fellow slave, who owes him a much smaller debt (yes, slaves lent money to slaves). When the second slave asks for mercy, the first denies it. The king, hearing about this interchange from fellow slaves, tosses the first slave to the torturers. It's not a pretty ending.

In ancient Israel, in Jesus's time, and today, unpayable debts create insurmountable barriers to families and to communities. If we forgive slights but do not forgive debts, there is no true family. At the same time, families hold each other accountable, so that one member does not take advantage of another. That's why, in the same chapter as the parable about the unforgiving slave, Matthew also speaks of internal discipline within the community. "And forgive us our debts, as we also have forgiven our debtors," should speak not only to our consciences, but also to our bank accounts.

RESCUE US FROM EVIL

26

Readings:
Matthew 4:1-11; Matthew 6:13;
Matthew 16:21-23; Job 1:6-12

And do not bring us to the time of trial, but rescue us from the evil one.

Matthew 6:13

The last line of the "Our Father" can be and has been read in two ways: rescue us from the evil one (i.e. Satan) and rescue us from evil (i.e. whatever view we have of evil, be it psychological or physiological). The former gives us the Devil, Old Scratch, Beelzebub, the supernatural enemy of "The Exorcist" and its various remakes, and somehow a force seen as (almost) equal to God; the latter gives us interior debate, traumatic experience, and the recognition that no supernatural evil could be as destructive as the evil we human beings do to each other.

For Jesus's listeners, the supernatural world was heavily populated: demons and angels all in various ranks, the devil, and God. The name *Satan* comes from the Hebrew term *satan*, which means *opponent* or *adversary*. Originally, it was not a name but a title, *ha-satan*, the satan, and it referred to a member in good standing of God's heavenly court (I am reminded of Hamilton Burger, the prosecuting attorney on the old *Perry Mason* show; he also usually lost). The satan is the supernatural figure who tested Job to see if he would remain righteous when all his blessings were taken away. This same prosecuting attorney shows up in Zechariah 3:1-2; here he is attempting to bring charges against Joshua, one of the early post-exilic priests.

The only time the Hebrew text gives us Satan, the proper name and the increasingly demonic figure, is in 1 Chronicles 21:1, where he incites David to take a census of the population. Since such numbering in antiquity was designed to determine taxation amounts and military draft, we can understand why some would see Satan's hand here. This text is actually a rewrite of 2 Samuel 24:1, where God provides the impetus.

By New Testament times, the supernatural, evil figure known variously as Satan, Beliar/Belial, Mastema, and so on had substantially developed. Now there was a malevolent, powerful force in the Garden of Eden, tempting Israel in the wilderness, and tempting Jesus in the wilderness as well. Despite Jesus's claim that he "watched Satan fall from heaven like a flash of lightning" (Luke 10:18), Satan's power is not diminished. His minions still possess people (hence the need for Jesus and his followers to perform exorcisms); according to Luke and John, Satan possessed Judas Iscariot.

Many of my friends believe in a literal Satan, a supernatural figure who, although already defeated, still is fighting a cosmic war with the earth and the bodies of people as the battlefield. I respect their view, even though I do not share it. I also worry when, on occasion, someone claims that Satan is the primary cause of temptation, or of evil, and so seeks an excuse for inappropriate action. "The devil made me do it" can be theological jargon for abdicating personal responsibility. Perhaps the reason I do not believe in Satan in the sense of a supernatural being is that I have seen the evil people do. I do not want people to use Satan as an excuse.

We do not need Satan for we do a good job of bedeviling each other. I appreciate Jesus's rebuke of Peter in Matthew 16:23. "Get behind me, Satan!" he tells Peter when the disciple rejects his announcement that he will suffer and die. Peter believes he is furthering the cause of the kingdom when he denies Jesus's statement (and the road to hell really is paved with good intentions). But Jesus calls out Peter as a stumbling block (the Greek for *stumbling block* is *skandalon*), an impediment to his mission. Like Satan's three temptations in the wilderness, Peter's exclamation of "Let it be merciful to you, Lord" (the NRSV's "God forbid it" is an overread; Peter does not mention God) presents a real temptation, since Jesus would prefer to be spared from the cross. We don't need Satan to tempt us; we do the job well enough on our own. Nor do we have to worry about Satan, for to worry about Satan is to diminish the power of God.

The more Christians saw Satan as the evil, supernatural rival of God, the less the rabbinic tradition did. Guided by the limited role of *the* satan in the Tanakh, rabbinic Judaism stressed not a supernatural evil to be overcome, but a human inclination to be harnessed. For example, one morning prayer cited in the Babylonian Talmud (*Berakhot* 60b) asks God, "May the good inclination have dominion over me and may the evil inclination not have dominion over me."

Whether we believe in a supernatural Satan or whether we recognize that the human heart has the tendency toward greed, egocentrism, selfishness, and a host of other "evil inclinations," we have a battle to fight. The Torah gives us the start; the Sermon on the Mount and other later Jewish interpretation advance the struggle in the right direction. And whether we believe in a supernatural Satan or not, we must recognize that we all have the potential to take his role and to resist it.

MAMMON

27

"No one can serve two masters; for a slave will either hate the one and love the other, or be devoted to the one and despise the other."

Matthew 6:24a

"Mammon, n.: The god of the world's leading religion. The chief Temple is in the holy city of New York."

Ambrose Bierce, The Devil's Dictionary *(1911)*

Human beings, as Jesus told Satan, do not live by bread alone but by the Word of God (Matthew 4:4). Bread alone, although necessary, is insufficient. And if we only had "bread," which then as now could function as a metaphor for money, then our hearts would starve. The point of the gospel is not to be the "breadwinner," the one who makes the most money, for if the goal is money, then money rules. If the goal is stuff, then mammon reigns.

Jesus tells a parable about a rich farmer who, because of a huge crop yield, determines to build bigger barns. He says to his soul, "Soul, you have ample goods laid up for many years; relax, eat, drink, be merry" (Luke 12:19). (I do worry about people who speak to their souls; they would likely be better off speaking to God.) That night, the fellow dies. Jesus concludes, "So it is with those who store up treasures for themselves but are not rich toward God" (Luke 12:21). The one who dies with the most toys most definitely does not win, at least not in the kingdom of heaven. The rich man worshiped the wrong god.

We all have multiple responsibilities: home and work; family and country; even church and state. Most of the time, these responsibilities do not conflict. At times, however, we need to make a choice: finish the work in the office or go to the child's baseball game? You can think of others.

This is not the type of choice to which Jesus speaks. To see what he means, we need to go back behind our English translations, and even behind Matthew's Greek, to Jesus's original Aramaic. Matthew 6:24 reads, "'No one can serve two masters; for a slave will either hate the one and love the other, or be devoted to the one and despise the other. You cannot serve God and wealth.'" Our first concern is that Jesus uses the language of slavery. The term for *serve* is *douleuein*, the infinitive form of the noun *doulos*, *slave*. Second, the term for *master* is *kyrios*, which in ordinary Greek means *lord* or *sir,* but is also the title for God (*kyrios* is the standard Greek translation for the Hebrew YHWH) or, in the New Testament, for Jesus. Finally, the term for *wealth* is, in Matthew's Greek text, the Aramaic word *mammon*, which means *money* or *wealth* or by extension *stuff*. To Matthew's Greek readers, *mammon* would have sounded like the name of a foreign god. Thus, Jesus asks not, "What do we own?" but "Who owns us? In whose house do we reside? by whose rules do we live? Who claims our loyalty? Who is our Lord?"

Trusting in our own amassed resources isn't just futile; it's useless in the way that the prophets warned that worshiping idols carved by human hands was useless (Isaiah 44:9-20; 40:18-20; 41:21-9). Trusting in stuff not only hinders our ability to find the way to the kingdom of God; it represents a turning away from that kingdom.

In our society, the syncretistic accommodation to mammon has even infiltrated theology, such as the so-called Prosperity Gospel (whose tenets logically extend to mean that, if success and wealth are rewards from God, then poverty and failure might be divine judgments). TV preachers who believe that private jets are essential to their ministries make easy and entertaining targets. Harder to confront is the call to self-examination. Do I want to be known as the rich person with bigger barns or do I want to be known as the person rich in compassion? At which shrine do I worship? Who owns me?

And then we realize, if our only master is God, then we are truly free to be what God intended us to be.

WHAT WE WEAR

28

Reading:
Matthew 6: 25-34

"And why do you worry about clothing? Consider the lilies of the field, how they grow; they neither toil nor spin."

Matthew 6:28

Buying new clothes for Easter remains a common practice: time for new pastels, new flowing skirts, new suits for the little ones. I also associated Easter with new hats, perhaps less from the store advertisements than from the wonderful movie, *Easter Parade*, with Judy Garland and Fred Astaire in their "Easter bonnets." Thank you, once again, Irving Berlin.

I didn't get new clothes for Easter, but connecting new clothes with holidays is not unique to Christian culture. When I was a child, my mother would always buy me new clothes for Rosh Hashanah. Because Rosh Hashanah occurs usually in September (the Jewish calendar is a lunar one, so the dates of the months vary), around the start of the school year, new clothes for the synagogue also meant new clothes for the new academic year. Going shopping for new clothes, along with that ever-important new lunchbox, remains a very pleasant memory. But I'm glad it's not the only one I associate with the holiday.

If the outfit becomes more important than the reason for it—to celebrate the resurrection of Jesus of Nazareth; to welcome the new year with its invitation to be better than we were the previous year; to embrace the new term with new things to learn—we have missed the point. Worse, that outfit will become outdated, or we will outgrow it, or it will eventually fray; like the toy we insisted on having one year but discarded the next, such external trappings are not where true meaning lies.

And yet those clothes do have something to teach us. For example, do we pay attention to the people who made our clothes? Do we know where our clothes were made and the conditions under which they were made? About whether the people who cut the cloth or stitched the seams worked in a fire trap or a sweat shop? Do we know how old these workers were or how much they were paid? While we were celebrating the good news of our holiday or our new semester, what good news did they receive?

We might also think of what we do with our clothes. Do we give them to the church or the synagogue secondhand store, to Goodwill, or to other programs that provide clothing for those who cannot afford it?

And in other cases, do we wrap up the new dress, the bow tie and jacket, the hand-knitted sweater, and save it for the next generation? I have saved the sweaters my mother-in-law knitted for my children; she no longer knits, as arthritis took away her dexterity and Alzheimer's took away her ability to follow the patterns. But the love she invested in those little gifts remains palpable.

Jesus tells his disciples, "Do not worry about what you will wear"—and he's right. At the same time, as we think about the lilies and the ravens, we might think about those who made our clothes. So too, he advises against worrying about food and drink. At the same time, we might think about those who provided us the food we eat and the drinks that quench our thirst.

And when we look at the outfit we may have saved, or tasted something that awakes in us special memories (like Proust, taking a bite of a madeleine and remembering times lost), we find that at least for a moment, as we reconnect with our past, worry is the last thing on our minds.

THE PRICE OF A SPARROW

Readings:
Genesis 1:26-31; Matthew 6:25-32;
Matthew 10:26-31; Psalm 139:1-12

29

"Are not two sparrows sold for a penny? Yet now one of them will fall to the ground apart from your Father."

Matthew 10:29

A few of my ecologically minded friends take issue with Jesus's suggestion that humanity is of "more value" than the birds. "All of the earth, every living creature," they insist, is of value. Academics are increasingly looking at "critical animal studies," the problems of "Speciesism," how to address socially sanctioned violence against animals (for example, the meat industry), meat as a sign of "cultural hegemony," and questions about how humans understand and treat the nonhuman animals. While the titles may sound like jargon (that is the way academics talk), we can learn a great deal from these approaches about ourselves and the animals around us.

On the other hand (already a human metaphor: other paw, other talon, other hoof . . .), I think Jesus is right on this one. Jesus is not denying value to creation; far from it! It may be rather that, in caring for the environment, the birds and the bugs, the rivers and the oceans, that we show our greatest potential. The nineteenth-century Orthodox Rabbi Samson Raphael Hirsch wrote that the function of human beings "is to show respect and love for God's universe and all its creatures."*

---

* Samson Raphael Hirsch, "Horeb : a philosophy of Jewish laws and observances" (2002). *East Collection*. 5. https://digitalrepository.trincoll.edu/eastbooks/5.

The Gospels don't provide much insight into Jesus's dietary habits, but it is safe to say that he enjoyed a good meal, whether with sinners and tax collectors, with Pharisees, with his disciples, with his friends Mary and Martha, or with thousands on the side of a mountain. (For this reason, even though he did a great deal of walking, I tend to picture him a little on the chubby side.) The Gospels do not state that he had meat at any of these meals; bread and fish and wine are the staples that receive mention. With the fish, he takes himself out of the vegan camp. However, absence of evidence is not the same thing as evidence of absence. It is likely he ate the Passover lamb when he went to Jerusalem for the pilgrimage festivals, and it is likely as well that the spread put out by those sinners and tax collectors was on the lavish side.

Consuming meat isn't necessarily incompatible with exercising careful stewardship over the creation that God pronounced good (industrial farming of animals raised for consumption is a different matter altogether). Nor does dominion license environmental destruction. To the contrary, the trees that God created, detailed in Genesis 1, are to be preserved even in times of war. Deuteronomy 20:19 mandates, "If you besiege a town for a long time, making war against it in order to take it, you must not destroy its trees by wielding an ax against them. Although you may take food from them, you must not cut them down. Are trees in the field human beings that they should come under siege from you?" Trees are not people: people can choose to make war, trees cannot. Therefore, the trees must be protected.

Animals must be cared for. To be a legitimate food source, the animal must be slaughtered in the least painful manner possible; one of the Noachide commandments, which according to post-biblical Jewish thought, all Gentiles (as is everyone descended from Noah) should follow is to refrain from eating a limb from a living animal.

The Price of a Sparrow

Every living thing is of value to God and, therefore, should be valued by human beings. But for now, at least, I'm placing the value of a human child over an animal or a plant. I'm also willing to revisit the question. One hundred years from now, or maybe sooner, we may learn that my ecology-centered friends have been right all along about the equal worth of all creatures.

THE DAYS
OF OUR LIVES

30

Readings:
Genesis 6:3; Deuteronomy 30:15–31:2;
Deuteronomy 34:7; Matthew 6:27

"And can any of you by worrying add a single hour to your span of life?"

Matthew 6:27

Years ago, I watched a soap opera called *Days of Our Lives*, and I still recall the opening line: "Like sands through the hourglass, so are the days of our lives." Time crept very slowly in Salem (I have no idea in which state this Salem was located), where the Hortons and the Bradys fought and loved and lived and, sometimes died (with a few returning as lost twins or imposters, and others being replaced by new actors). I worried about those characters. I also worried about missing an episode. I now have other things to worry about.

Nevertheless, those sands through the hourglass inexorably flow from top to bottom. Jesus says we cannot add more time than the time we have been allotted, but that is not true. Healthy choices in lifestyles, new medications, good healthcare can all add hours, even years, to our lives. I take Jesus's comment here to be one that reminds us of our finitude. I am of an age where those in my cohort, friends and fellow students and family, are realizing our own relationship with time: some of us are retiring; others are fighting failing bodies; some of us have died.

Instead of worrying about death, the entire biblical tradition helps us refocus by telling us to celebrate life. Instead of fighting death, we may come to realize that the time is less to fight than to embrace. Our bodies will inevitably fail us at some point. Instead of fighting when fighting will no longer avail us, we can refocus. We can prepare. If we follow the guide Jesus offers in the Sermon on the Mount, we shall be prepared. But that is only the first step, for there is more to the Bible than the one sermon, and there is more to tradition than the Bible. For example, in *Pirke Avot* 2:10, Rabbi Eliezer advises, among other things, that we repent one day before we die. Since most of us will not know that day, we can always take this healthy precaution.

More, we know that we will not get everything done. There will always be one more book to read, or cheek to kiss, or scarf to be finished. The good news is that we do not have to finish everything. Moses got his people to the borders of the Promised Land; others will take his place and help them enter. Jesus will ascend into heaven, and it will be the responsibility of his followers to carry on his word and his work.

We know that death is not the end of our story. The Jewish tradition and the Christian tradition both proclaim resurrection of the dead. But they offer more. The stories we continue to tell, about Moses and Jesus, our family and friends, keep their memories alive. The actions we take in their names help complete what they began. When the time comes for all of us, we are not alone. We are always in the memories of others, and we are always in the sight of God.

TO SEEK AND SAVE THE LOST

Readings:
Matthew 10:5-11; Matthew 19:16-30;
Luke 19:1-10

31

"Take no gold, or silver, or copper in your belts."
Matthew 10:9

Jesus's warnings about laying up treasures on earth and his teachings about the impossibility of serving both God and material things apply to everyone. However, he takes aim particularly at the rich, and I suspect that Matthew's target audience are the wealthy followers of Jesus, mostly Gentiles, in the Greek-speaking world.

The Sermon on the Mount is flanked by images of wealth. Matthew begins with a royal genealogy and introduces high-end gifts with the magi, who present to the newborn king gold, frankincense, and myrrh (Luke gives us shepherds, who apparently show up empty-handed, although open-hearted). When Jesus instructs his disciples on how to engage in their missionary work, he tells them, "'Take no gold, or silver, or copper in your belts, no bag for your journey, or two tunics, or sandals, or a staff'" (Matthew 10:9-10a; see also Mark 6:8). There's no reason to ban gold or silver if the disciples have no slush fund; there's no need for the concern for two tunics if the men only have one. Only Matthew describes Joseph of Arimathea as a "rich man" (Matthew 27:57).

There are well-off disciples, such as Mary, Martha, and their brother Lazarus; not all folks have "costly perfume" (John 12:3) or homes big enough to set up a banquet for Jesus and the twelve who follow him. Luke informs us that Zacchaeus, the chief tax collector for Jericho, was rich despite his insistence, "Look, half of my possessions, Lord, I will give to the poor" (Luke 19:8). The NRSV has added that "will" before "give;" the Greek verb for "give" is in the present, not the future tense. Zacchaeus has already been giving to the poor. Jesus does not convert him from greed to generosity; Jesus gives him the public forum in which he can correct the people's negative stereotype of him. Not all rich are greedy; not all rich are uncaring.

Matthew knows that wealthy disciples will read this Gospel; Matthew may even be counting on them to compensate the scribes who will copy it (or, because we should be honest about how economics worked in the first century, provide what is literally slave labor). When asked why he dines with tax collectors and sinners (i.e. the rich; those who promote self-interest rather than community welfare), Jesus responds, "Those who are well have no need of a physician, but those who are sick. Go and learn what this means, 'I desire mercy, not sacrifice.' For I have come to call not the righteous but sinners" (Matthew 9:12-13). Greed is a disease, and it requires healing. Wealth is a trap for sin, and it requires generosity.

Wealth is often a disease of which those afflicted are unaware. When Jesus encounters a rich man who asks him, "Teacher, what good deed must I do to have eternal life?" (Matthew 19:16), Jesus does not tell him that this is an ill-phrased question. Eternal life is not something that can be gained simply by donating a can of soup to the food pantry or putting a dollar in the collection plate. Jesus tells him to follow the commandments, and the fellow then demands, "Which ones?" Again, the question is unfortunate. Avoiding murder but engaging in adultery and robbery is not quite the path to the kingdom Jesus had in mind.

Jesus continues to show patience. He starts by listing part of the Decalogue, the ten commandments: "You shall not murder; You shall not commit adultery; You shall not steal; You shall not bear false witness; Honor your father and mother" (Matthew 19:18-19) and he adds Leviticus 19:18, "You shall love your neighbor as yourself." Anyone who knows the Decalogue—and Jesus's original audience, including this rich fellow, would have known the Decalogue—would know that Jesus shifted the commandments around. Honoring parents is the end of the first table; "do not murder" begins the second, the list of "thou shalt nots." The commandment concerning the parents is in the wrong place. What should have been there—and what fellow Jews, including the rich man, would have known—is the last of the ten commandments: "You shall not covet your neighbor's house; you shall not covet your neighbor's wife, or male or female slave, or ox, or donkey, or anything that belongs to your neighbor" (Exodus 20:17).

The rich man insists he has kept them all and wonders what he is still lacking. Here Jesus builds a fence around that last, missing commandment. From "do not covet" Jesus advises complete divestment: "'If you wish to be perfect, go, sell your possessions, and give the money to the poor, and you will have treasure in heaven; then come, follow me'" (Matthew 19:21). The rich man does not become a disciple. As we hear this story, we do well to think about the things we covet, and then, if we can, start working on the fence.

JUDGE, BUT DO NOT BE JUDGMENTAL

Readings:
Matthew 7:1-2; Leviticus 19:15; Romans 2:1-6

32

No Justice, No Peace
(political demand and lament)

The term "judgment" shows up over two hundred times in the New Revised Standard translation of the Bible. Frequently, it has the connotation of punishment, as in Malachi 3:5, "Then I will draw near to you for judgment; I will be swift to bear witness against the sorcerers, against the adulterers, against those who swear falsely, against those who oppress the hired workers in their wages, the widow and the orphan, against those who thrust aside the alien, and do not fear me, says the LORD of hosts." This type of judgment is fine, in my view. It's about time those false swearers, those economic oppressors, those who deny justice to the widow, the orphan, and the alien, saw what true justice looks like.

Yet frequently as well, it is the covenant community that finds itself on the receiving end of this judgment. Speaking of the northern kingdom of Israel, Hosea 5:11 announces, "Ephraim is oppressed, crushed in judgment, because he was determined to go after vanity." We should not wish on others the judgment that we would not wish on ourselves.

There are many areas in life that are judged, whether we like it or not, or even whether we are conscious of doing it or not. We judge how we look in the mirror in the morning; we judge others by their appearance, their clothing; we judge people by how they speak (I find myself losing respect for people who misuse pronouns, as in "She gave the gift to him and I," or who end sentences with prepositions). With all this judging, we keep making mistakes. We misjudge our looks; we misinterpret the signals of others; and we often mishear how others use language.

Because it is so easy to misjudge, Jesus builds another fence by commanding, "'Do not judge, so that you may not be judged'" (Matthew 7:1), and then he continues by speaking of how, if we do judge, then we need to be prepared to be judged by the same standards. The command does not mean, however, that we should only be bystanders, for our responsibility is also to offer just judgments and to pursue justice. Hence the cry, "No justice, no peace."

Both Leviticus and Deuteronomy require impartiality in rendering a judgment. But determining what constitutes justice is a tricky thing. Rather than think the verse is an argument against affirmative action, or against giving the poor person a bit of leeway in repaying a debt whereas insisting that the rich person pay up immediately, we do better to look more carefully at the Hebrew. It reads, literally, "Do not make inequity in judgment. Do not lift up the face of the poor and do not honor the face of the great; with justice/righteousness (*tzedek*) judge your neighbor" (Leviticus 19:15). Otherwise put: when it comes to justice, we should neither romanticize the poor as incapable of doing wrong, nor should we presume that the prominent citizens are to be treated in a more formal or respected way.

Paul makes the same point for his Gentile readers in the Roman assembly: Do not judge others by standards you do not yourself uphold. Know that there is a final judgment, and that God will judge everyone, and repay everyone, not according to what they profess, but "according to each one's deeds" (Romans 2:6). Those deeds include judging others.

Judge, but Do Not Be Judgmental

It is a good idea to start the day by looking in the mirror, and instead of judging ourselves by impossible standards, repeat, "This is the image and likeness of God." Then, throughout the day, look at everyone else and repeat the same words. They apply to victim and offender both, and they apply to us as well.

THE CANAANITE WOMAN

Readings:
Matthew 1:1-5; Matthew 15:21-28;
Mark 7:24-30; Matthew 7:6-7;
Hebrews 11:31; James 2:25

33

Then Jesus answered her, "Woman, great is your faith! Let it be done for you as you wish." And her daughter was healed instantly.

Matthew 15:28

Matthew 15 recounts Jesus's encounter with a Canaanite mother of a demon-possessed daughter; Mark 7 tells more-or-less the same story, but in Mark's version (7:26) the woman is "a Gentile, of Syrophoenician origin" (the Greek literally reads, "a Greek, a Syro-Phoenician by birth"). The stories are variations on the same themes: crossing ethnic boundaries; addressing needs; overcoming resistance.

In Mark's version, the woman encounters Jesus in a home, and she begs him to perform an exorcism for her daughter. He responds, "Let the children be fed first, for it is not fair to take the children's food and throw it to the dogs" (Mark 7:27). He is telling her, "Wait your turn—I've much more work to do in Israel." In Matthew's version, his rejection is sharper, "It is not fair to take the children's food and throw it to the dogs" (Matthew 15:26). No "be fed first" here; in Matthew's version, Jesus gives the woman no reason to hope.

Worse, in each version, he refers to the woman as a dog. This is no more a compliment in antiquity than it is today. We may hear in the background the Sermon on the Mount: "Do not give what is holy to dogs; and do not throw your pearls before swine, or they will trample them under foot and turn and maul you" (Matthew 7:6).

Don't waste your resources, Jesus tells his disciples. Why would he think aiding this woman would be a waste?

For Mark, the woman's description—"a Greek, a Syro-Phoenician by birth"—suggests an upperclass status. Her identity markers further suggest that she is the enemy; Josephus notes, "for you cannot but know that there was not any one Syrian city which did not slay their Jewish inhabitants, and were not more bitter enemies to us than were the Romans themselves" (*War* 7:367). Despite her being an upperclass woman from a group that oppressed Jews, she gets what she needs, for Jesus eventually yields to her request. Do not throw what is holy to the dogs, but *make sure your assessment of others is correct.*

Jesus has assessed her actions and her words. In terms of action: she does not respond to insult with insult or with violence. In terms of words, she shows Jesus the true import of what he said: "'Sir, even the dogs under the table eat the children's crumbs'" (Mark 7:28); the term the NRSV translates as "sir" is *kyrios*, literally, *lord.* Jesus is impressed by her retort, and he says so, "For saying that (Greek: "on account of this word"), you may go—the demon has left your daughter" (Mark 7:29).

For Matthew, the woman is a Canaanite, a descendant of the people who opposed Israel in antiquity. Again, why would Jesus use his resources to help her? But wait: Matthew has already mentioned two Canaanite women in Jesus's genealogy: Tamar and Rahab. We know that Tamar was more righteous than her father-in-law Judah, and Rahab was more righteous than the spies sent into Jericho. We know this Canaanite woman is going to use her wits to achieve what she needs.

The Canaanite woman is in a more difficult situation than her Syro-Phoenician counterpart. First, Jesus ignores her plea; then he tells her that his mission is only to the lost sheep of the house of

Israel. Calling her a dog and denying her his help comes third. But she persists: "'Yes, Lord, yet even the dogs eat the crumbs that fall from their masters' table'" (Matthew 15:27). The translation misses a stark point in the Greek: the word translated *Lord* (*kyrios*) is the same word that gets translated *masters* (*kyrios*, in the plural). She places herself in a more subordinate position than the Syro-Phoenician woman.

Whereas in Mark, Jesus praises the woman's "word," in Matthew, he commends her "faith" and performs the exorcism. Whether her faith was in Jesus's ability to heal, in her ability to get him to acknowledge her, in his role as "lord" or "Lord," we are not told. But when we go back to the Sermon on the Mount, we find another reason why she prevailed. Following the comments about pearls before swine, Jesus states, "'Ask, and it will be given you; search, and you will find; knock, and the door will be opened for you'" (Matthew 7:7).

If we are shut down or shut out because of who we are, where we live, our background, economic status, ethnicity, religion . . . If we are seen as dogs, then we should not respond with insult. Like this Gentile mother, we should model the Sermon on the Mount's "third way" of avoiding the escalation of violence while maintaining dignity.

And if we see others as dogs, as not worth our time or our resources, then we clearly need to look again. Responsibility rests with all parties—those who have and those who need—and there is enough bread to go around.

DO *FOR* OTHERS?

Readings:
Matthew 7:12; Matthew 22:35-40

34

"In everything do to others as you would have them do to you; for this is the law and the prophets."

Matthew 7:12

The Golden Rule troubled Immanuel Kant, and it has troubled philosophers before and after him. "Do to others" suggests that the others are objects upon whom we impose our own wishes. We know how we want to be treated, but it would be a mistake to assume that others want to be treated the same way.

I have a dear friend who once invited me to work with her in her garden; for her, digging and planting, weeding and watering are spiritually renewing. I'd rather have a root canal than spend time on my knees with the dirt and the bugs. I'd rather be in the library than in the garden; for her a day in the library would be a day in hell. For the Golden Rule to work, we need to respect diversity, have empathy, and refrain from imposing our will on others.

When I hear the expression, "Do unto others" or, in colloquial English, "Do [this] to them," I get a negative impression. I don't want to be "done to" or "worked on." Perhaps we might rephrase the Golden Rule by changing the preposition from "to" to "for," as in, "Do *for* others as you would have them do *for* you." Doing *to* may well be imposing something unwanted or treating a person as an object; doing *for* is providing a service.

"Do for others..." is a better formulation, but it still has problems. The helpful in-law who rearranges the kitchen cabinets for the newlyweds may have the best of intentions; the newlyweds will have other thoughts when they can't find the oregano or when they do find the meat tenderizer. Doing *for* also risks the problem of patrons and clients. If you do something "for" me, I will likely feel the need to reciprocate; that feeling is not based on a legal system, but it is just as psychologically powerful as knowing one has to repay a debt.

There are numerous other philosophical arguments against the Golden Rule. Rarely, however, do the philosophers engaged in such critiques look to the Rule's biblical context. For Matthew, we cannot understand the Golden Rule unless we consider it in relation to the Torah and the Prophets, and by extension, to the Scriptures of Israel.

In the Sermon on the Mount, Jesus summarizes these Scriptures by the Golden Rule. Later, when he is teaching in the Temple, he summarizes these same Scriptures by citing Deuteronomy 6 on loving God and Leviticus 19 on loving the neighbor. We now have guides for the Golden Rule: It must conform to what the Torah mandates and the Prophets teach; it must be enacted with love. To understand the Golden Rule, therefore, we need to understand Leviticus and Deuteronomy as well as Genesis, Exodus, and Numbers.

Jesus gives two summaries of the Law and the Prophets. There are others. The Babylonian Talmud (*Makkot* 24a), offers additional summaries of the 613 *mitzvot* (Hebrew for *commandments*) worth considering:

- Micah 6:8 got the list down to three: "He has told you, O mortal, what is good; and what does the LORD require of you but to do justice, and to love kindness, and to walk humbly with your God?"

- Isaiah 56:1 gets the list to two: "maintain justice, and do what is right."
- Amos 5:4 offers one verse: "Seek me and live."
- Habakkuk 2:4 also offers one verse: "the righteous live by their faith." Here Paul agrees (see Romans 1:17).

No summary of ethics, of scripture, of the gospel is sufficient. An abridged novel might get us the plot, but it will not give us the opportunity to savor the words. Separating the Sermon on the Mount from the rest of Matthew robs it of its myriad nuances. And taking the Golden Rule out of the Sermon risks turning words designed to love the neighbor into words that will create harm or hate. To understand the Golden Rule in its fullness, we have to look at the rest of the Sermon on the Mount, the rest of Matthew's Gospel, and the Law and the Prophets.

THE ROAD LESS TRAVELED

Readings:
Matthew 7:13-14; Matthew 13:3-9;
Deuteronomy 30:11-30

35

"Enter through the narrow gate; for the gate is wide and the road is easy that leads to destruction, and there are many who take it."

Matthew 7:13

As Deuteronomy draws to an end, and with it the life of Moses, the great prophet lays out two options for the people: one route leads to life and the other to destruction. "Choose life," Moses says, "so that you and your descendants may live, loving the LORD your God, obeying him, and holding fast to him..." (Deuteronomy 30:19b-20a). Choosing life means following the Torah, which in later Judaism came to be known as the "tree of life." In synagogues today, when the Torah scroll is returned to the ark after being read, the people sing the words of Proverbs 3:18, "She is a tree of life to those who lay hold of her; those who hold her fast are called happy." The next lyric is the previous verse, "Her ways are ways of pleasantness, and all her paths are peace" (v. 17).

Moses reminds the people that following the path that leads to life "is not too hard for you, nor is it too far away" (Deuteronomy 30:11). It is not in heaven; it is given to the people, who now have the responsibility to interpret it, and to live into it. "It is in your mouth and in your heart for you to observe" (Deuteronomy 30:14).

In times of peace, following the Torah is not too hard, and it never was. Although a number of Christians have told me that they find the idea of 631 commandments intimidating (at best), I am usually able to assure them that following the Torah is easy. It is no more difficult to follow the Torah than it is to follow the laws of any modern state, and there are plenty more laws in the local system than there are in the Torah and its two thousand years of interpretation. The commandments (*mitzvot*) are easy to follow, but one has to work at it. One has to be sure that the food is kosher; one has to choose to stop working on the Sabbath; one has to be comfortable with the choice of remaining a member of a minority group.

The difficulty enters not because the commandments are too demanding, but because our own egos and own desires are too compelling. It's easier to assimilate than it is to maintain cultural identity; it's easier to think of our immediate needs than it is to think of the long-term needs of the planet; it's easier to say "peace, peace" than to notice the places where peace cannot be found.

In times of bigotry, of forced assimilation, of hatred, following the Torah can be difficult. Refuse to eat pork and the empire will kill you, whether that empire be that of Antiochus IV Epiphanes in the second century BCE or the kingdoms of Spain and Portugal during the Inquisition in the fifteenth and sixteenth centuries. Circumcise your sons, and you may doom them and you, as was the case in Nazi-occupied Europe. Wear a kippa and you may be attacked on the streets of Paris, Brussels, or Kansas City.

Years ago, when our children were very young and still students at Nashville's community Jewish elementary school, we picked them up from the school and drove directly to the airport. The plan was to catch a flight to Florida and to be with the grandparents for a long weekend. When we arrived at the terminal in Palm Beach, my in-laws were there to greet us. After the hugs and the kisses, my mother-in-law took me aside. She was concerned that our son, direct from school, was still wearing his kippa. "Take it off him," she asked—she was worried that he would be ridiculed. I assured her that he would be fine and he was. And she eventually was as well, especially when Alexander told her he could recite the entire Hebrew alphabet.

Jesus recognizes both the benefits and the dangers in speaking of the narrow gate. In times of peace, the narrow gate is found when we love others as we love ourselves and when we follow the Golden Rule together with the rest of the teachings of scripture. In times of strife, the narrow gate is found when we do what we should do rather than what we are told to do by false prophets.

There is no guarantee, nor even a statistical probability, that taking the narrow path to the narrow gate will lead to health, wealth, and happiness. Such a promise would be a variant of the Prosperity Gospel, and I don't want to go there. Turning the other cheek makes one vulnerable to being slapped again; extending mercy to an enemy risks being repaid with a knife in one's back. Being recognized as a member of a minority group can get you killed. Be merciful anyway. Be a peacemaker anyway. Celebrate your identity anyway. Choose this narrow gate and you'll have a foot already in the kingdom of heaven.

FALSE PROPHETS AND GOOD FRUIT

36

Readings:
Matthew 7:15-23; Deuteronomy 13:1-4;
Jeremiah 6:13-15; Micah 3:5-12.

"Not everyone who says to me, 'Lord, Lord,' will enter the kingdom of heaven, but only the one who does the will of my Father in heaven."

Matthew 7:21

From earliest times, people have been warned against false prophets, and from earliest times, those false prophets have found a ready audience. Warnings extend back to Deuteronomy 13, which issues proscriptions against "those who divine by dreams" and those who "promise you omens or portents." Deuteronomy is not concerned with the *how* the prophets obtain their information; it is concerned about the content of that vision. Tell the people to worship strange gods and you're a false prophet.

We can hear how this image might play out in later times. The Babylonians and Persians, the Greeks and the Romans encouraged the people of Israel to assimilate, to be just like everyone else in the empire. A few Israelites, or Judeans, or Jews concluded assimilation was a good idea. They told their friends and neighbors, "We should worship the same way as our neighbors; we can worship our God, but let's call him Marduk or Mithra, Zeus or Jupiter." Deuteronomy warns: these prophets of assimilation are false prophets. Do not listen to them.

Along with introducing strange gods, the easiest way to tell a false prophet from a true one is that the false prophet offers all good news without any demands. False prophets are the gatekeepers of the wide gate that leads to destruction (Matthew 7:13) and the real estate agents who sell plots of sand (Matthew 7:26).

Jeremiah was particularly harsh toward those prophets who kept affirming that the nation was living in *shalom* when there was no peace; there can be no peace when "the wounds of my people" remained untreated. Jeremiah's concern was less the looming Babylonian conquest than it was the failure of the nation to take care of its most vulnerable citizens. Jeremiah's words hold the same truth through the ages. Those who say "peace peace" when there is no peace, no *shalom*, are false prophets.

Micah's acerbic denunciation of the prophets who "cry 'Peace' when they have something to eat, but declare war on those who put nothing into their mouths" (3:5) is even more visceral. It's an easy move from his false prophets to the evangelists who siphon "love offerings" from the gullible faithful. But such evangelists are an easy target. For both Micah and Jeremiah, the problem is not "them"; the problem is "us"—yes, all of us.

Politicians who today say we are the greatest, wisest, smartest, most technologically adept people, but who fail to notice the hungry and the hurting fall into the category of false prophets. Religious leaders who proclaim that "we are saved" when, as Jeremiah puts it, "from the least to the greatest of them, everyone is greedy for unjust gain; and from prophet to priest, everyone deals falsely" (6:13) fit into the same category. But the prophecy gets harder, for any of us who are perfectly content, who say "peace peace" because we have locks on our doors, a state-of-the-art burglar alarm, and a full stomach, and who ignore the needs of others, we too are false prophets. Those who are living the dream will be, as Jeremiah, Micah, and Jesus all proclaim, in for a very rude awakening.

False Prophets and Good Fruit

In the Sermon on the Mount, Jesus warns his disciples against false prophets, and he does so with the marvelous image of wolves in sheep's clothing (Matthew 7:15). Some of these predators, Jesus says, not only will prophesy in the name of God, they will even perform miracles. Miracles do not prove messianic status; miracles are primarily for show. The kingdom of heaven is found less in the circus or on the stage, and more in the shelters and the food pantries and in the houses of worship where both love of neighbor and love of God prevail.

Jesus provides a ready identification, albeit a mixed metaphor, for false prophets: You can discern the true shepherds from the wolves, Jesus advises, by watching for the fruit they bear. And if he needed to make it any clearer, Jesus spells it out in Matthew 7:21: the way into the kingdom of heaven is doing the will of the Father.

FATHERS AND MOTHERS

Readings:
Matthew 23:8-12; Mark 5:21-24, 35-43;
Matthew 7:7-11

37

"Is there anyone among you who, if your child asks for bread, will give a stone?"

Matthew 7:9

Those of us of a certain age might recall the TV show, *Father Knows Best*. It aired from 1954 to 1960, and then it went into reruns through the 1960s. Robert Young, who would go on to play the beloved Marcus Welby, M.D., was the father who knew best, Jane Wyatt the wife, and the children were played by Elinor Donohue ("Princess"), Billy Gray ("Bud"), and Lauren Chapin ("Kitten"). This Anderson family lived in "Springfield," well before the Simpsons took out a mortgage there.

Father Knows Best presented the ideal American family; it was for many viewers clearly fiction. Not all families were financially stable, had two parents, had a dad who "went to work" and a mother who "stayed home" (as if the mother were not herself "working"). Not all parents are wise and not all families escape the lure of drugs and alcohol (Lauren Chapin became addicted to drugs; she is now a Christian evangelist). Sometimes we look for role models, for the perfect families, on the television. We also do well to see how real families function, and here the Gospels become a helpful resource.

For those of us who try to be the best parents we can, and who sometimes come up short in the "Knows Best" category (we will), the

Gospels offer some relief. We are all in this life together, says Jesus, and no one has to bear the full burden of protecting, deciding, or supporting. In Matthew 23:8-12, Jesus instructs his followers, "You are not to be called 'rabbi' (in the sense of master-teacher; he is not speaking of ordained clergy)" because "you are all students." That is, we learn from each other. More, "call no one your father on earth (in the sense of king-master), for you have one Father" who is the one in heaven. Nor do people in his community have "instructors" (in the sense of leaders; the term here is unique in the Bible), for the Messiah is leader enough. Jesus is speaking of titles—rabbi, father, and instructor are all honorifics—and saying: no need for that. Community membership is not about receiving honor, but to be in service to all.

It is in such service, not just to their own biological children, but to all the children of God, that fathers and mothers both appear. Joseph, who is not Jesus's biological father, protects Mary and the child first by taking them from their home in Bethlehem of Judea to Egypt and then by relocating the family to Nazareth in Galilee. Sometimes Jesus himself steps into the father role: he not only raises the child of Jairus and his (unnamed) wife from the dead, he also takes over Jairus's role as head of the household by determining who enters and leaves the home. He is also the one who insists that the revivified girl be given something to eat. I would like to think that at this point, Jairus and his wife—exhausted by their care for this very ill daughter—appreciated the help.

Despite all the biblical "father" language (which gets increased by those translations that read "was the father of" rather than "begat" for the genealogies in Matthew and Luke), we should not overlook the mothers in the text, for sometimes they are the ones who know best. More, they are also responsible for protecting, deciding, and supporting. The Canaanite woman of Matthew 15 knew what was best for her demon-possessed daughter; the women in the genealogy (Tamar, Rahab, Ruth, and Bathsheba) knew what was best for themselves and their families.

The mother of James and John did the best she could for her sons. She approaches Jesus and asks if her two boys could sit at his right and left hand when he enters his kingdom. But Jesus gently tells her that such honors are not his to grant; those honors are prepared instead by his Father (see Matthew 20:20-23). Later we learn that the two at his right hand and his left hand are the other two men, crucified next to Jesus (Matthew 27:38). I appreciate her advocacy, but in some cases, it is best to let the children make their own way in the world rather than either rely on parental pushiness or, worse, think that they are incapable of achieving anything on their own.

We parents do our best when we feed our children bread and eggs, not stones and scorpions, when we teach our children the importance of service, when we seek healing for them, and when we demand justice for them. More, we do well when we have the help of our community: when we have the courage to ask for it and the courage also to accept it.

BLESSED ARE
THE DOERS

"Everyone then who hears these words of mine and acts on them will be like a wise man who built his house on rock."

Matthew 7:24

The old hymn that begins, "How firm a foundation, ye saints of the Lord, is laid for your faith in his excellent Word," may well be based on the last section of the Sermon on the Mount. The third verse even evokes flood imagery: "When through the deep waters I call thee to go the rivers of sorrow shall not overflow." For the hymnist, the foundation is Jesus; if the reference to the "Word" in the first couplet did not make this clear, the second couplet does when it asks, "What more can He say than to you He hath said, to you who for refuge to Jesus have fled?"

But that's not quite what Jesus is saying in Matthew 7.

The Gospel of John describes Jesus as the *Logos*, the Greek term for *word* and a circumlocution for the sacred name of God. Some Aramaic versions of Genesis translated by Jews around the time of Jesus—the technical term for such as translation is a *Targum*—describe God as creating by his *memra*, Aramaic for *word*. Thus, Jesus the Torah teacher evokes both the Scriptures of Israel (what his followers would eventually call the Old Testament) and his interpretations of them, such as the extensions. And he is doing even more.

In the Sermon on the Mount, Jesus goes beyond acknowledging the importance of the word, whether that word involves the Scriptures or his own person. His emphasis is on the word *built*, a verb that involves action. He does not say that all people who hear his words are like the wise who build their houses on solid rock; he commends only those who hear his words and then *act* on them. The Greek underlying the NRSV's "act" is *poieō*, the standard verb for *do* or *make*, a word that appears over five hundred times in the New Testament. In the Sermon on the Mount, it appears first in relation to those who "do" the commandments and teach them (5:19); it is the verb in the Golden Rule (7:12); it refers to those who do the "will of my Father in heaven" (7:21).

Even more, the Greek translation of Genesis 1:1 records *poieō* as the verb: "In the beginning, when God *created* the heaven and the earth..." (italics added). To act on the divine word is not simply to sing the hymn or even put the money in the collection plate. To act is to create, which is what building a house is, as architects and building contractors, carpenters and plumbers, painters and interior decorators, and the host of others it takes to build a house already know.

Jesus had been talking about dual loyalties: to God and to mammon, or to the kingdom of heaven vs. that very tempting kingdom of earthly delights. We can import that teaching into the saying about the two builders, the one who built on a solid foundation and the one who built on sand. But that is not all the verses suggest.

Jesus has just been speaking about judgment, about who will "enter the kingdom of heaven" (7:21). The entry card is not those who "say 'Lord, Lord,'" no matter how heartily they sing in the choir or praise Jesus on a daily basis. Rather, Jesus is speaking to those who create, construct, work (yes, that dreaded term, "work") for the building of the kingdom. To turn chaos into order, to bring forth grain from the ground, to steward creation, to build a home that is full of love—that's what it means to act, to build, to do. The Hebrew term for this is *Tikkun Olam,* which means *to repair the world.*

As for the blueprints: they are already present: the Torah and the Prophets, as understood by Jesus's teaching. There's an old *midrash* (*Genesis Rabbah* 1.1) that I remember hearing when I was a child. It goes something like this: When God decided to create the world, he decided he needed a blueprint. So he looked in the Torah, and there on the first page he read, "Then God said, "Let there be light"; and there was light" (Genesis 1:3). So God said, "Let there be light." And so creation began.

The midrash is paradoxical, as many good stories are. But we nevertheless know where it leads: act as if your life depends on the Word of God (however you understand that expression) and you'll withstand any storm. Don't just exist but create, for you are also in the image and likeness of the Creator. Don't just speak, do, for words not followed by actions are like the wind that either signals a blowhard or, worse, topples others. Wisdom is found in informed creativity. Go build (on) the firm foundation.

CIRCUMCISED HEARTS

39

Readings:
Matthew 7:15-20; Jeremiah 31:33-4;
Matthew 21:28-32; Deuteronomy 30:6;
Luke 13: 6-9

"In the same way, every good tree bears good fruit, but the bad tree bears bad fruit."

Matthew 7:17

Repeatedly, Jesus says that actions speak louder than words. We judge the quality of a tree by whether it bears any fruit and what kind of fruit it produces. It is impossible, Jesus tells his hearers, for bad trees to yield good fruit. Grapes don't grow from thorns, nor can thistles produce figs.

Jesus tells a parable about a landowner who orders his gardener to chop down a fig tree because for three years it has failed to bear fruit. The gardener arranges to get the tree a reprieve: "'Sir, let it alone for one more year, until I dig around it and put manure on it. If it bears fruit next year, well and good; but if not, you can cut it down'" (Luke 13:8-9). I do wonder what that gardener had been doing while the tree failed to produce, but he does finally recognize the threat to the tree (and perhaps to his job) and so gets to work. A gardener who doesn't care for plants has the job title, but doesn't deserve it.

What does not bear good fruit now may produce abundantly in the future, if it gets help. An individual may not bear good fruit, but with community support—a little pruning here; a little fertilizer there—that individual may blossom. Here Jesus suggests the role of the community: before we write someone off, before we conclude that she is a thorn or he is a thistle, make sure we have provided all the resources to help those individuals bear good fruit.

Jesus tells another parable about two brothers—brothers are a staple of stories in the Scriptures of Israel—whose father asks them to work in the family vineyard. One brother at first refuses, but then changes his mind and works. The other obediently promises to do the work, and then bails. Which son, Jesus asks, did the will of his father? The question is rhetorical. Bearing good fruit is what counts. The major concern is not what we say, but what we do. Making the promise but not following through looks good at first, but it produces nothing. Worse, it creates false expectations.

We can even extrapolate further. The major concern is not *when* but *that*: some are called late to the vineyard, some come to the realization of responsibility later than other; some regret their first comments and go about bearing fruit. Otherwise put, some are late bloomers.

As for that son who promised to go, but did not, Jesus has a few words regarding him as well. Ideally, what we say and what we do will be harmonious. We might pay more attention to the words we use, especially in prayer. We promise to "forgive debts" or "forgive trespasses," but we continue to hold grudges. We promise to love our enemies, but we are more inclined to drop bombs on them. We speak of God's will being done on earth as it is in heaven, but we come up short in the "doing God's will" department. This is not how it should be.

Deuteronomy 30:6 promises, "The LORD your God will circumcise your heart and the heart of your descendants, so that you will love the LORD your God with all your heart and with all your soul, in order that you may live." That concern for loving God comes from an earlier verse in the same book. Deuteronomy 6:5 proclaims, "You shall love the LORD your God with all your heart, and with all your soul, and with all your might." We'll only be able to fulfill that proclamation when our hearts are in line with our heads and our bodies.

As we wait for this metaphorical heart surgery, we can prepare for it, just as we might change our diet or our exercise habits in order to prepare for a medical procedure. How can we develop our spirit so that what we do is matched by how we feel, that our hearts and our heads and our bodies are all working together? When we start following the narrow path the Sermon on the Mount describes, doing the will of the Father becomes easier and easier; it becomes something we want to do all the time, because it makes us feel better.

The Sermon on the Mount tells us how we recognize good trees. They bear good fruit. But we can extend the metaphor. From the parable of the fig tree in Luke 17, we know that what looks like a dead tree might just be dormant; what looks like an unproductive plant might, with some coaxing, yield abundantly.

Good trees are known by their fruit, not by their leaves, just as disciples are known by what they do, not what they say or what they promise. When one's heart is in harmony with God's will, then what Paul calls "the fruit of the Spirit"—love, joy, peace, patience, kindness, generosity, faithfulness, gentleness, and self-control (Galatians 5:22-23)—naturally and inevitably sprout from the branches. We need not only consider the lilies of the field and the ravens in the air; we might consider the fruitful trees of the faithful followers.

TEACHING WITH AUTHORITY

Readings:
Matthew 7:28-29; Luke 4:17-20; Nehemiah 8:1-8

40

Now when Jesus had finished saying these things, the crowds were astounded at his teaching, for he taught them as one having authority, and not as their scribes.

Matthew 7:28-29

The Sermon on the Mount is Jesus's longest uninterrupted speech—three full chapters in Matthew—recorded by any of the Gospel writers. His comments during and after his Last Supper in John's Gospel fill four chapters (14-17), but there are a few interruptions, such as when Thomas asks him where he is going and how the disciples can know the way (John 14:5); thus, Jesus's famous comment, "'I am the way, and the truth, and the life. No one comes to the Father except through me'" (John 14:6) is actually the answer to a question. Thomas may be asking for some special knowledge, or spell, or esoteric teaching that would gain him access to the Father (we see hints of such concerns in the famous Gospel of Thomas). But in John's Last Supper discourse, Jesus tells Thomas that access to the Father comes from the Son, who in the beginning was with God and who is God.

Of all four Gospels, John's Gospel is most interested in Christology, in the understanding of Jesus as both human and divine. Of all four Gospels, Matthew's is most interested in pedagogy, in the teachings of Jesus and about Jesus. In Matthew's signature section, the Sermon on the Mount, Jesus begins with the Beatitudes and concludes with the call to be doers of God's will and not merely hearers of God's word. Matthew does not record what the disciples, the direct addressees of the Sermon, were thinking. But Matthew does give the reaction of the crowds who were, at a distance, listening. They are astounded, not just by his insights into the heart of the Torah but by the way he teaches with authority. To the crowds, Matthew says, Jesus does not sound like the scribes they were used to hearing.

There were several types of teachers at the time: the scribes were the ones who preserved traditions, drew up contracts, knew legal precedents, and otherwise had at least a modicum of literacy. The Pharisees drew upon what the Gospels call the "tradition of the elders" (for example, Matthew 15:2; Mark 7:3,5—the term for "elders" in Greek is *presbyteron*, which is where we get the term *Presbyterian*. I keep picturing John Calvin debating with Jesus, but I digress), ways of understanding how the Torah was to be practiced, much as law codes today tell us what "all men are created equal" or "the right to bear arms" means. The Teacher of Righteousness led the group, possibly Essenes, that gathered at the Dead Sea; John the Baptist taught his followers, and so on.

The scribes had templates, earlier documents on which to depend. Jesus knows the Torah, but he is not reading from a scroll, or even from the *Cliff's Notes* (although I like the idea of "*cliff* notes" to a "sermon on the *mount*"). Rather, Jesus signals that he is relying on his own authority when he begins six separate teachings with the formula: "You have heard that it was said...but I say to you..." (Matthew 5:21-48).

He speaks of what they had heard "said," and not what they had heard "read." Here we may come to a difference between Jesus and the scribes that biblical scholars debate but that I have found makes a number of people in the pew uncomfortable.

Why does the crowd compare Jesus to the scribes, and not to the Pharisees, the Essenes, or any other group? Here is one possible answer, and I leave it only as a possibility. What distinguished scribes was literacy. And so the question comes: could Jesus read? According to Luke's Gospel, he is handed the scroll of Isaiah (the full Isaiah scroll from Qumran has 54 columns; it's huge) and he finds the place where Isaiah writes, "The Spirit of the Lord is upon me..." Provocatively, Luke does not say that Jesus "read" the text. Some scholars therefore wonder whether Jesus was more or less illiterate.

In working with both children and adults suffering from dyslexia, and in teaching students whose parents are functionally illiterate, I raise this question. In the modern West, literacy is essential; in the ancient world, scribes were present for contracts and law; some people had the skill of reading, but most even in the Jewish world did not. And so the Sermon on the Mount forces us to ask where authority lies: in book knowledge or in action?

Authority should belong to the doers of the word and not with those who hear or teach. More, in our age when we place so much value on education, those of us who have the advanced degrees or the fancy letters after our names (another nod to literacy) must always recognize that true virtue, creativity, and acting in the image and likeness of God is not found ultimately in the intellect or in the academic training, but in the heart and the will.